AS THINGS WERE

Canon Arthur Bax wrote these memoirs as a very old man, after a full life as both a town and country parson. His working life, which began with his ordination in 1893, saw many changes, which he faithfully recorded, taking us back to a time long gone. His accounts of the countryside and its inhabitants and of times of social change are a delight to read and will appeal to all those who enjoy a nostalgic trip into the past.

AS THINGS WERE

Canon Arthur N. Bax

Edited by Clare Vines

CHIVERS LARGE PRINT
BATH

British Library Cataloguing in Publication Data available

This Large Print edition published by Chivers Press, Bath, 1994.

Published by arrangement with Mrs M Vines.

U.K. Hardcover ISBN 0 7451 2074 1
U.K. Softcover   ISBN 0 7451 2085 7

Photoset, printed and bound in Great Britain by
Redwood Books, Trowbridge, Wiltshire

PREFACE

In July 1988, before we moved from Petersham to Richmond, Stephen Napier Bax brought me the manuscript of 'As Things Were' asking me to read it. I put it in a drawer and didn't come back to it 'til after we had moved, and sadly, Stephen had died. He was my Uncle Arthur's eldest grandson. I liked the book so much that I decided to have it printed for the family, as a thank you to my uncle and cousins for making my first memories so delightful.

My uncle, Canon Arthur N. Bax, wrote these memoirs as a very old man, helped by Clemency, and Romola, and his grandson Stephen. When I first remember him, he was Rector of Maperton. In late July 1914 my father, mother, brother and sister and I, were having a holiday in Weymouth. My father was in the Royal Marine Artillery and his ship was in Portland Harbour. On the night of July 28th his marine servant threw gravel at my parents' bedroom window, as a signal to my father to rejoin his ship, which sailed that night under sealed orders. War against Germany was declared on August 4th and my mother took us to live with my uncle and his family at Maperton.

Our Grandmother, Mrs Bonham Bax,

otherwise Granny Bax, was there because, tragically, Auntie Diana had died nearly two years before, leaving her five children motherless. The two eldest, Stephen and Clemency, who were twins, were fourteen, Oliver was twelve, Romola six and Anthony five. My brother must have gone back to Kelly College for the Autumn term, but he got into Woolwich when he was still sixteen, so he was only at Maperton when on leave.

The Rectory was a home to so many in the two world wars—the Homfrays and the Lawrences, and the New Zealand cousins who were mainly Gordons in the Great War, and in the second world war during 'Doodle Bug' time my sister Jean took our sons John and Jeremy there—Romola was there too, as her husband was away with his regiment. My niece Antoinette Roxburgh used to visit as she was at school nearby. Stephen Napier Bax was there as well, in his holidays.

Life with Uncle Arthur was highly organised. Prayers were at eight am, in the dining room, attended by all the family, the maids, and the visitors. After breakfast, Romola, Jean and Anthony had their lessons with our uncle in his study. I was too young at the age of two, when we arrived, to take part, so I was turned out to play in this paradise of a garden, which covered several acres, and was beautiful. It included two flower gardens, with lawns and great trees—one a wonderful old mulberry tree, to which we slung our hammocks when sleeping out. There was a large kitchen garden, stables, a farm yard, duckpond, pig sties, and an orchard where cows grazed and pigs roamed. Also, there was a large field and a paddock, where Col. Ridley, the squire, grazed some of his hunters and kept a pony and a donkey for us children. Romola, Jean and Anthony learned to ride on the pony, bare back, and the donkey was consigned to me. There were also two goats who supplied milk for the household and whose kids were usually killed for the table. Their skins were made into bedside mats. There were three cats, a Blue Persian called Cosy and her two half Persian sons, Tiger who was long haired and gentle, and Nimrod, who was huge, fierce and unfriendly and truly a mighty hunter.

My uncle believed in visiting and getting to know his flock and helping them in every way he could. For example, he used to dig the gardens of the women whose husbands were at the war. He never had a car, but went everywhere by bicycle or train. Often he would take his family with him, me on the bar of his bicycle and the rest on their own small bikes. Clemency, Stephen and Oliver were boarders at the two Sherborne schools. We played a lot of games with my uncle, such as croquet and rounders, and later on when we were older, golf. People were the most important things in my uncle's life, and although he was outwardly undemonstrative, we all knew he cared for us. He liked to feel we all helped in some way. There were the most lovely haymaking parties, the older boys and Clemency were very efficient and we little ones had a really good time, but probably got in the way. There were people at the rectory I haven't mentioned. There was Bessie the cook, whom we all loved. I had bantams and she used to make the cock dance to her singing on the back of the kitchen settle. She looked after the poultry and I remember helping her to catch hens for the table and watching her wring their necks! How could I?

There was Mrs Dyke who came to help in the house and whose son Willy was the gardener's boy and young enough to play with us. Anthony bought Mrs Dyke's cottage when she died—his step daughter Josephine lives there now. She is church warden and organist. Uncle Arthur would have been so pleased.

Sadly, all my uncle's children have died, and all but Stephen are buried in the family grave in the churchyard at Maperton. Looking into the rectory garden after Romola's funeral in the early summer of 1990, I found nothing changed, it looked so beautiful.

Maperton was a very small village. Life revolved around Col. and Mrs Ridley at Maperton House, my Uncle Arthur at the rectory, and the farming community.

Col. Ridley was a squire in the old tradition. He was the kindest and most generous man I have ever come across. He hated to be thanked. At that time he was acting MFH of the Blackmore Vale Hunt, which we children used to follow on his pony, taking turns of course. After any of us had been 'blooded' (a ceremony to mark the first occasion of being in at the kill) we would hear the clatter of something being posted through the letter box, and a hunting crop would arrive for whomsoever had earned it.

Passing the old stone breaker in a shower of rain, the Colonel noticed that he, the stone breaker, had nothing to keep the weather off, so next time he passed that way, he threw a brand new macintosh on to the pile of stones, not pausing to be thanked. Col. Ridley rode almost everywhere, and I remember conversations with him, from a very different level—he never made me feel I was the baby. He gave a penny once to stop me howling; it worked! He gave us a giant cracker at Christmas stocked with presents for each one of us. We used to pull it, boys one end girls the other, and at Easter, an enormous egg was delivered, with chocolates inside. He had no children of his own. I remember his coming to see us at Bath in 1918, at my grandmother's house, and my brother was there. He had been wounded in the leg and Col. Ridley rolled down his own stocking to show the great bump on his leg where he had been wounded in the Boer War and they compared notes. He always arrived in church on Sunday with a large retriever, which lay in the aisle, all through the service, perfectly quiet. There were times at Maperton when he showed a firm hand. On one occasion the choir boys, of which my cousin Anthony was one, threw sweets across the chancel to each other. The Colonel rose in his wrath and boxed their ears—there and then.

There wasn't the same sort of country life at Radstock, as it was a mining town. Clemency had her studio in the rectory and it was a joy to watch her carving. She did a lot of work for her father's church—the sun dial and the memorial screen, and I used to watch her restoring the bosses from the oak knees, supporting the rafters. Her work with gold leaf was fascinating.

I should like to thank all those who have helped to put 'As Things Were' together: Jane Napier Bax, Stephen's wife, her daughter Deborah and her son-in-law Michael for their unfailing support, Helen Bax for the photographs of Uncle Arthur and

Aunt Diana, Clemency's daughter Diana Reid and her daughter Janet, Bettine Lawrence, Ann Douglas-Cooper, John, Christopher and Betty Bax.

I should also like to thank those who have taken photographs of the churches at Maperton and Radstock; our son Stephen and his son, Mark; our son Simon and our great nephew Bruce Roxburgh. Many thanks are also due to my brother-in-law, Ralf Vines for finding drawings of St Mary's Church, Moseley, Birmingham, where he is Church Warden and where my Uncle Arthur was Vicar all those years ago.

Clare Vines
Richmond, Surrey
December, 1990

CHAPTER ONE

SUNDERLAND

It was the Festival of St. Thomas 1893. The Ordination, which had been held in Durham Cathedral was over. We had dined in the Castle, and had bidden farewell to the Bishop (Dr. Westcott) and to Cecil Bontflower, his chaplain, and I now stood dressed in a clerical frock coat on the platform of Durham Station. I was on my way to Sunderland to the Curacy of St. Thomas's, Bishopwearmouth, where my vicar was to be Canon Reginald Talbot who was later Dean of Rochester. How strange and uncomfortable I felt on that draughty platform in the dim light of a late December afternoon amid a small crowd of businessmen and workpeople! My clothes troubled me. An old Norfolk jacket and riding breeches was the costume that I liked best, but that was not my only distress. Everybody seemed to be staring at me. The black frock coat was however soon laid aside and used only on special occasions such as a wedding party.

Much worse was awaiting me. I was about to enter a new world, quite unlike that of which Bede dreamed when he lay dying in the Monastery at Jarrow, a few miles away on the Tyne.

The Parish of St. Thomas's Bishopwearmouth was a very small one—no more than the size of two big fields. Its area was but 64 acres, but its population was 7,200. The church was at the upper end of the parish in John Street, not far from the central station, in what had been a residential quarter, but was now given over to offices. Between that and the old parish of Sunderland and the docks, then a very poor district, lay the densely populated part of our parish in which was a very large building known as St. Thomas's Church Institute, that was to be the centre of my work. There on Sundays I was to hold a Bible Class in the afternoon and a Service in the evening and on week nights to carry on clubs for young fellows and for men, who met there—the Men's Club upstairs and the Boys' in the big room on the ground floor.

My two rooms were in a house almost adjoining, from which my bedroom looked out on Sussex Street, and my sitting room on the Borough Road, which was cobbled. Through the long working hours of the day the noise of the wheels of the lorries on the cobbles on their way to and from the docks was incessant. Between us and the Institute was a tiny yard.

I was to be looked after by a prematurely

aged woman and her stalwart but stumpy daughter, Bella. I think Bella's mother was a bit crazy. The house, it appeared, had a bad reputation. It had been inhabited, I was told, by a lady named Mary Ann Cotton, a local celebrity, who attained fame and at that time figured in the Chamber of Horrors, for she had qualified for a place by specialising in the murder of husbands, but that information came to me later.

Mary Ann Cotton won more than local celebrity. She was committed for trial in October, 1872, on the charge of having poisoned her four husbands and four children. She was executed at Durham in the following March. There is apparently every reason to believe that Mrs. Cotton poisoned altogether more than twenty people, including her own mother and her previous husbands and all her children by them.

From time to time Bella's mother would appear and in an awed voice tell me that she had just seen Mary Ann Cotton crossing the yard, leading a child. Her voice when she spoke of the lady was subdued and very impressive.

At other times she would have a fall out with her daughter. It is nearly sixty years now since I inhabited the house, but there is still imprinted indelibly in my memory the picture of Bella, a short lass stoutly built with muscular red arms, pinning her mother

3

securely to the wall in a corner with a broom, the head of which was planted firmly against the maternal stomach. The pose of Bella was that of a rugby forward entering a scrum. The mother was nearly beside herself with rage. Her screams were awful, but though her arms worked like a windmill, she could not reach her daughter and was helpless.

The cooking was of the quality that might be expected. I ventured to entertain my predecessor to lunch and to celebrate the occasion I told Bella's mother to obtain a duck. After a few minutes wrestling with his portion of the inedible bird, my guest looked up and said, 'Well! I have never seen before good food so spoiled,' and laid down his knife and fork in despair.

Happily the reign of Bella and her mother was short. They were succeeded by an old couple, who had been in good service. From that time on I had nothing to complain of in the housekeeping. They were excellent.

Sunderland was in 1895 one of the most overcrowded towns in England. According to the Census returns, overcrowding in Gateshead affected 40 per cent of the population; in Newcastle 35 per cent, Sunderland 32, Plymouth 26, Halifax 21, London 19, Birmingham 14, Liverpool 10, Bristol 8, Nottingham 3, Portsmouth 1.75. Sunderland had the third worst record in England.

In Sunderland the three East End parishes were typical not only of overcrowding, but of how and why overcrowding took place. Of that I shall say more later, but first I will describe my near neighbours, for some of whom I retain a great regard.

With the Christmas holidays a hard frost had set in. I rather enjoyed it. I was well clad and Sunderland coal makes a bright fire. There was no shortage in those days and coal was very cheap, about 12/- a ton, I think.

The Festival began in the true north country style, with a deal of drinking and thus the money saved for Christmas was quickly exhausted. New Year followed with 'first foot' celebrations, a legacy from Scotland. The frost still held, day after day for weeks on end, and that meant that the mass of my parishioners were out of work. Most of my neighbours were employed in the shipbuilding yards, and a frost soon laid them idle. While riveting the plates on the frame of a ship, the men had to work on staging, where they could not with safety swing a hammer in a frost. Among my immediate neighbours were many men who had held well paid jobs, but through intemperance had dropped out of their unions. While in work they made quite good money, but normally they saved nothing. Very soon owing to the stoppage of work through frost they were penniless, and their credit at the shops, always scanty, was at an end.

An idea came to me. I would start a woodyard in the cellars of the Church Institute. It was a comfortable place in those bitter days, for the furnace kept it warm. I talked to my vicar about it. He was not enthusiastic; he knew too much of these things. He had been curate to Canon Moore Ede, afterwards Dean of Worcester, a leader in social matters at Gateshead. He promised me a few pounds from the Poor Fund. (Ours was a rich congregation, for the church was still attended by families who had formerly lived in John Street in the houses which had now become offices.)

To the vicar's subsidy I was myself prepared to add something, and I hoped that by the sale of wood in addition, we might keep going for a time, without becoming insolvent. I procured wood for cutting up and some implements and set a few men on to work who had big families. I purchased a barrow and appointed a rather feeble man, who had many children, to take charge of it. His home was run by a nice wife, who faced the impossible task of maintaining it and a rapidly growing family on his earnings. His name was Corkin.

My employees all seemed pleased and the first day passed happily, but not strenuously.

The next morning more men came to ask

for work, and I set on two or three additional hands. The third morning there was a queue stretching up the Borough Road waiting for my appearance. The fame of my effort had spread. It was very embarrassing, and I learned how difficult it is to turn men away who are seeking work and have a family dependent on them. I told Corkin, who brought our barrow around to deliver wood at some houses where I had obtained orders, and in due course I sat down to my lunch. As I was about to begin I looked out of the window. There in front of me was Corkin sitting on his loaded barrow. Full of rage I hurried outside and asked him in no measured tone, why he did not get on with his work. 'I can't face that hill,' he said, 'I am faint. I have not had any food since yesterday.' My anger died away and a sense of shame followed. Corkin ate my lunch that day and after that he sold the wood and I was full of distress as I thought of my blindness.

My next lesson was also a simple one. I had to pay the men—I gave a small sum for a short day—two shillings. We could not afford more, but 2/- would buy quite a lot of food in those days, if it were well laid out, and I had no money to do better. At the end of the first day I had the change and paid them myself. The next day we had ten on and I had no change. I appointed a foreman and in my inexperience there seemed to be an easy solution. I would give a sovereign to the foreman; let him take the men with him, get the change and pay the men. They seemed dissatisfied and hung about. I asked what was the matter. They explained that if they went to a shop the money might be retained for their debts, if they went to a pub, the publican would expect them to have a drink. The difficulty was easily met but important. They accompanied me to a shop and received from me, each man his money, and I always had enough change ready after the lesson they had taught me.

I struggled on with my woodyard until the frost broke. It cost me more than I had contemplated spending, but the money was certainly not wasted. It helped a small number of families in my immediate neighbourhood, and looking back I have no doubt that it made a great difference to the way I was received by my neighbours. I had become at once one of themselves. I knew their troubles and felt for them.

Sussex Street where I lived had seen better days. It probably dated from about the middle of the nineteenth century. The houses had been built for fairly well to do people. They had basements, a ground floor, and two floors above. The basements were virtually cellar dwellings. At the time I knew it, there were four families normally in each house. The gardens had been partly built over with poor insanitary hovels. The population of Sussex Street was strangely mixed. Most of the men should have been earning good wages as I have already said, but many had dropped out of their unions. Drink generally was the enemy. Here and there were really first rate people, and also here and there criminals. Few, I think, should have been poor except in periods of trade depression. A neighbour of poor Corkin, who lived in a garret, had been at Eton and Oxford. Drink had brought him low and generally when I saw him, he would weep tears of self-pity. His wife, if she was his wife, was a very good woman and she had a very well brought up little boy—whether his child or not, I cannot say. She was a regular attendant at our Mission Service and she always brought the boy with her. They never sought for help. After a time I got in touch with his people and they made provision for them. One day they bade me goodbye and set off for the South and I knew them no more.

The class of tenant in the different houses varied greatly. In the house beyond the Institute the top room was then occupied by a man who had done time for false coining. On the next floor below the man had been convicted of burglary. Below that was an Irish hawker, who when drunk, which was frequent, would try to put his wife's head

9

through the panel of the door. In the cellars were an old couple who had served a sentence for procuring young girls. Next door to them were a very different set of people. One young couple were a blacksmith and his wife. He was one of the very best fellows I came across in my three and a half years in Sunderland. He was on the committee of our Men's Club. I remember him saying to me as we stood discussing something at the front door of the house in which he lived, 'Well! Mr Barks' (I was always called that locally) 'I don't call a man a man unless he has principles.' He was a strong trades unionist.

In the cellars was another interesting family called Goodrich. The eldest boy was the most attractive young fellow in the Boys' Club. He became interested in Economics, and seeking a book on the subject at a venture, was given to begin on Adam Smith's 'Wealth of Nations'. No doubt in time he read what could fire him, for in the year I went to Sunderland, Robert Blatchford of 'The Clarion' wrote 'Merrie England', of which more than a million copies were sold. My copy seems to have disappeared, but here are some words from another of his books, 'Not Guilty, a Defence of the Bottom Dog'—'The case for the bottom dog should touch the heart to the quick, for it affects the truth of our religion, the justice of our laws, and the destinies of our children. Much golden eloquence has been squandered in praise of the successful and the good; much stern condemnation has been vented on the wicked. I venture now to plead for our poor brothers and sisters, who are accursed of Christ and rejected of men.' It was good rhetoric, no doubt, but strange words to apply to 'the Friend of publicans and sinners'.

If my dear old Bishop, Dr. Westcott, ever read Robert Blatchford (and I think that almost certainly he did) he would have felt all the more the truth of his conviction that 'The distribution of wealth in England was perilous'. Words I have heard him use many times. Rich people have cause to be thankful that the wars, and what followed, have brought about a great levelling of wealth.

Young Goodrich prospered, married a nice girl from our Girls' Club and, so far as I know, all went well with them.

It was in Sussex Street that I enjoyed hospitality for the first time in that parish. I called on some cellar tenants half way up the street. I explained that I was the new curate and had called to make their acquaintance. The lady told me that their name was Hope and invited me in. Seated by the fire were a tall muscular man and the two Misses Hope, his daughters. There was scarcely any furniture, but a chair was found for me. The others sat on sugar boxes. The man was a riveter in the shipyard, who had fallen out of his Union from the usual cause. They were just going to have tea and invited me to partake. I accepted the invitation and I was offered a kipper, which I declined, but accepted a piece of bread and butter. The only drinking vessel was a stone jam pot, and being the guest I was offered the first drink. Thus we began an acquaintance, which so far as I know, bore no fruit, except a general friendliness and goodwill, but that is certainly not to be despised.

At another cellar dwelling on the same side I arrived at an unpropitious moment, and had a very different experience. The door was opened by a stalwart Irishman, who was a bit in liquor and I stumbled down three steps into a half dark room to find its occupants seated round a pail of beer. They looked at me without any sign of welcome and gave me no invitation to be seated, nor was there in fact any vacant seat. I did not choose to run away, so I sat down on the table. Then the man who had opened the door rose, and laying his hand on his breast, said, 'I have Jesus Christ in my heart,' I replied, 'I wish you had Jesus Christ in your habits.' Whereupon he resumed his seat, and silence fell upon the company. It was clearly of no use sitting on so I rose and said I was afraid that I had come at an inconvenient moment so I would look in another time, and left amid general silence.

I saw a good deal of my host after, for we were near neighbours. He was a big fellow who had been in the Scots Guards and afterwards in the Police Force, but had been discharged for the usual failing. For some reason in his queer way he seemed to have taken a fancy to me which expressed itself in an unusual form. If he was a bit into liquor, which he generally was, he invariable tried to embrace me, while announcing in a loud voice that I was his best friend. Later on we fought a successful ward election on the housing question. He, like many others, had promised to give his vote to our candidate. Again and again during the polling day he approached me to request release from his promise and became pathetic about the good beer he was losing. It was after seven o'clock in the evening when I last saw him that day and he was still seeking release. Probably he was by 8 p.m. too drunk to vote at all, but our friendship was unbroken.

My opposite number in Sussex Street led me a pretty dance one night. The husband and wife were Londoners. The man had one of the good trades; his wife had been a board school mistress, a decent nice educated woman, borne down by circumstance. He drank, and when he was drunk he was a first class beast. They had seven children. One

13

night, it had just struck eleven, and I was lately back from the Men's Club. I had had a cup of cocoa, had read for a few minutes, and was just going to bed, when there was a noise of feet outside the window and a low hesitating knock at the front door. Outside were clustered the ex London school teacher and her seven children. She was crying and the children pressed around her. 'My husband has turned us all out of the house,' she murmured. Her utterance was broken with sobs of shame and misery. 'Can you find us some shelter for the night?' she said.

I took them into my warm sitting room and left them in front of the fire, while I went to see what I could do. I found an old woman nearby who was ready to receive them but I had to compensate her heavily the next day for the insects which, she said, they had left behind, but the insects were probably natives.

Poor mother! That would, I think, have been the last straw, if she had ever known the sequel. No doubt the hostess was making the worst of things, with a view to justifying her bill, which was not that of a philanthropist.

Sometimes the summons was for help. Here is a typical one. The noise of someone running, a halt on my doorstep, a smart rap on the door, and a summons, 'Please come round at once, Mr. T. is murdering his wife.' It was only a short distance to their rooms.

When I arrived, the house was quiet. I went upstairs and entered without knocking. The wife was in one chair breathing heavily and her face running with blood. She held a saucepan in her hand—a poor weapon. She should have chosen something better than that. He was sitting opposite her, drunk and glaring. He had used his fists and heavy boots. It did not seem worthwhile to say anything at first, so I drew some water in the saucepan and swabbed the wounds a bit. Very soon she was crying and he remorseful. There was no occasion to say much or to draw morals. The fury had died out; the tears had come. Their son, a boy of about sixteen years of age, was one of the best lads in my Club and Bible Class.

The Club, with its Bible Class and Mission Service, was the most effective and the main part of my work, but I am persuaded that neither would have prospered without visiting, getting to know parents and homes and surroundings. Visiting is, I suspect, too much neglected today, perhaps owing to the shortage of clergy.

My mornings I had largely at my own disposal, and until I began to suffer from the strain I was able to do some reading. I almost always like people as I get to know them and get interested in their lives, even if they are scoundrels.

At times when the children were about

('the bairns' I should say), Sussex Street could be quite a cheerful place, especially if a hurdy gurdy were there. It was delightful to see the children dancing to its music. I have never lost my affection for that instrument, which we never hear now. It is a real loss in a poor district. I never see children dancing in the street to the wireless as they used to dance to the hurdy gurdy, but perhaps that is because I do not now live in Sussex Street.

The children of Sussex Street bloomed early, but while they bloomed, they were very attractive. Sometimes the games did not lack imagination. I remember one day, as I emerged from my lodgings, hearing terrible cries from a cluster of children assembled around a lamp post. Hotfoot I hurried to the spot while the cries became more and more anguished as I drew near. What on earth are you doing? I cried. Then the cluster parted and exposed to view, a boy tied to the lamp post, whose cries had become more piercing and pitiful as I drew near. Beside him was another boy drawing the leash of a whip through his fingers. There was a universal outburst of laughter at my expense, to which the victim contributed his part. They cried as I halted, 'He's Uncle Tom, we're playing Uncle Tom's Cabin and we're flogging him.' The victim turned a laughing face towards me. Then the Overseer wielded the lash once more, and Uncle Tom lamented. I doubt if

16

the original Uncle Tom ever bellowed like his representative in Sussex Street.

II

The Church Institute in Sussex Street was the centre of my work. In the big room on the ground floor the Lads met every week night. Upstairs the men met in a smaller room in which billiards was the chief attraction. On Sundays we had a Bible Class there in the afternoon and on Sunday evenings a service in the big room, where on week nights the Lads' Club met.

The Lads' Club involved most work, but I had one reliable helper, William Metcalfe, a master carpenter, to whom I owed much. He used to arrive somewhat later than I did and was most efficient. He played the harmonium at prayers, and on Sunday evenings, and gave the choir such training as they had. He attended the Bible Class, and played our hymns. Sometimes he contributed to our discussion, but there as his words invariably were the same on each occasion he was not so valuable. He would lay a Bible in the palm of his hand and pointing to it with the other, he would say: 'You see that book. That is a Bible. Now people have been aspecking at that book for hundreds of years and there you see it still.' In spite of his limited theology and strange

17

way of expressing it, he was to me a most loyal and valued helper, and I do not know what I should have done without him.

The Lads' Club closed at 9 p.m. and then I went upstairs to the Men's Club. We had a reliable Committee there and before 9 p.m. it was sufficient for me just to look in once or twice while I was wanted in the Boys' Club below the whole time.

It was quite different downstairs. The members included gangs from the street corner. Church clubs are normally one of two types—the net or the fold. Our Lads' Club was a net 'that gathered in of every kind'. Those who belonged to a street corner gang were of a rough type. There were no tests of membership. Even in my Bible Class there were Roman Catholics. All that we asked as a condition of membership was that they should conform to the rules while present. The Club was closed with prayers, which gave me an opportunity to speak to those who attended. If they wanted to avoid prayers at the Boys' Club they could do so by leaving at 8.30 p.m. Prayers were at 8.45 p.m. Hardly any left before. We secured discipline at prayers by Metcalfe playing the hymn in front, and I took the prayers from behind. Under that arrangement the order was good, and prayers, mainly extempore, were brief, simple and to the point and not infrequently topical. A fold of course is a very different matter. It is generally composed of men or lads who are real members of the Church, and sometimes a fold is very successful in doing what they set out to do. For entry into our Men's Club there was a test for members of the Lads' Club, who had reached a suitable age and wished to join the Men's Club—had he learned to behave himself? Until he had learned that lesson he, whatever the age, was not eligible. That rule, I think, worked well. The men had no desire for rowdy members and would not put up with them.

The Lads' Club was pretty big and it was difficult to get an efficient committee. In despair I tried including, as an experiment, a gang leader or two, but though their physique commanded respect and they had leadership, it was not a success. The first one I put on the Committee very quickly disappeared for a month, and arrived back from his unexplained absence with very short hair. His comrades gathered around him, apparently congratulating him upon his return to public life, and he seemed sheepish. I always liked him and I think that he liked me. One day when he had been guilty of some enormity, I pitched into him severely, and to my consternation he burst into tears. We got his bosom friend off to sea as a stoker in the Navy and shortly after we were told that he had been put in irons.

My dear old Bishop looked in one night quite unexpectedly; I had never even dreamed of such a possibility. Clog dancing was going on. We gave him a chair and he became interested as he watched it. Some of the performances were very good. Suddenly the Bishop began to quote Homer:

'Skilled in the dance, tall youths, a
    blooming band,
Graceful, before the heavenly minstrel
    stand;
Light bounding from the earth, at once
    they rise,
Their feet viewless, quiver in the skies:
Ulysses gazed, astonished to survey
The glancing splendours as their sandals
    play.'

His visit was a great success. The members realised that that remote and hitherto almost mythical person, the Bishop, was interested in our club in Sussex Street. The action was one that widened the Club outlook and made my task easier. Bishop Westcott was of the same opinion as my other Bishop, Dr. Ridding, 'that a visit to a small place is often in its effects of more importance than a visit to a big.'

One year, when employment was scarce, half a dozen men were assisted to emigrate to Canada. I forget who organised the experiment, I think it was the Quakers. One of the party selected to go was a member of our Club; he was a man with a strong attachment to billiards. It was a shock when a few weeks later, on entering the Men's Room, I saw taking aim for a stroke a well known form. He had returned already. He 'did not like the country' he told me. I believe that the other five did the same. They preferred Sunderland, and casual labour, to opportunity, which promised success to those who would face hardship and hard work. The money had been found in vain.

One of the most popular of the Club activities was boating. We had at first one and later two boats on the Wear. In the summertime they were greatly used on Saturday afternoons and in the evenings after work. A row up the Wear, past the shipbuilding yards, and past Lambton Castle, was not to be despised.

Our Sunday service was hearty at any rate. The choir were all members of the Boys' Club. Their average age was probably about sixteen, and they were in number about a dozen or so, strong young fellows who attended well. They strode in from a classroom in single file. They wore no surplices or cassocks, and they sang according to their power and light, very heartily. They certainly led the congregation, and such as it was, it responded well to the lead.

By the door handing out the books was a constant helper, a grey haired man, prematurely old in appearance, who had a history, and like many to whom the light has come suddenly, he looked back on his earlier life as a time of deep depravity. He had more than once pointed out to me the spot in Coronation Street, the shopping thoroughfare of my district, where his 'call' came to him. He was that evening already half seas over and stood on the threshold of another pub, when an inward voice, which he looked on as the voice of God, said to him, 'Will you go to Hell for a glass of beer?' From that hour he was a changed man. Never again did he enter a public house, and whereas in his former life he was given to 'rioting and drunkenness', now his pleasure was to seize opportunity for doing good. He left the sea and became a street scavenger under the Corporation, and had attached himself to our Mission—that was before I knew him. More than once he has told me about what happened, which gave him more pleasure than any other happening in his life. He was working in the road in a poor quarter, when his attention was attracted by a girl, who was evidently in sore trouble. He went up to her and asked her what was amiss. She told him that she had run away from home and fallen into bad ways and was miserable, and durst not return home. He found out who her people were, visited them, and was the means of restoring her to her family. In due course she married happily. Auld stands to me as a type of the humble saint. That rescue had happened some years before I knew him.

As I think of my friends in Sunderland, there is one other that I must recall. On a shelf in our drawing room is a copy of Richardson's *Clarissa* in eight volumes, a seventh edition (1774) in the beautiful binding of that period—of leather stamped with gold. The first volume bore the name of the possessor, but that has been most carefully erased. It is a keepsake. It was given to me by a middle aged lady who lived in two rooms in a street, which was on the borderland between respectability and slumdom. She was a dipsomaniac, but so nice and kindly between attacks. I value the volumes for her sake as well as for the beauty of the books. They keep her memory green in my recollection. I never learnt her name.

These crowded alleys were difficult to work. Partly because the tenants changed so frequently, but people were friendly and helpful. On one occasion I wanted to find a man called Smith. A gang of boys and young men stood at the street corner, where Golden Alley met Coronation Street. I asked if anyone could show me where the man I sought lived. A lad stepped forward and offered himself as a guide, and hurried me down the evil-smelling alley. He halted before a door on the right, rather more than half way down, and said laconically—'Second floor.' I thanked him and entered. It was pitch dark within, and I stretched out my arms, feeling for the stairs. Suddenly a hand grasped my arm and a voice said 'Stairs.' The hand guided me and I began to climb. Whether my guide was male or female I know not. As I went forward I was conscious of brushing past another person. At the top of the second flight we halted and the hand had rapped on the door. I was released and heard my guide descending. It was an uncanny happening but I was grateful to my unseen guide and I can say that these street corner gangs never failed me.

On another occasion I was less fortunate. I had been visiting on the first floor of a house, and as I left I thought that I might as well go and see who lived above. I ascended a few steps in the utter darkness when suddenly I went through the stairway. The boarding had been torn up for firewood, and I found myself dangling in mid air, saved by my arms, which had been extended for guidance by touch in the darkness. It was a nasty experience.

'I hear that last night they found another man dead in Golden Alley,' I remarked to

Hennigan, an Irish Roman Catholic, nearing twenty years of age, a member of our Club, and of my Bible Class, a rough customer but quite decent. 'Yes,' he replied, 'I heard something about it, too, but I did not pay any heed. You must expect that sort of thing at this time of year.' It was Christmas time. Actually it was the sixth death of the kind during one Christmas and New Year season in our district. Hennigan spat and we parted. With his hands deep in his trouser pockets, he walked slowly with rolling gait down Coronation Street, and I turned up it.

Golden Alley was typical of the network of slums and alleys quite near to the house in which I lived. They lay between the High Street and Coronation Street and had a common origin. In old days the land they stood on was gardens that belonged to the shops in either street. The alleys were of a general pattern. At the High Street end you entered them under an arch which was lit by a lamp. From Coronation Street a cart could just enter each alley. I could in many places touch the wall on either side if I stood with outstretched arms. The houses had three floors and the courtyard behind was normally built over. The alleys, through the circumstances of their construction and the disregard of all sanitary rules, must be regarded as a typical slum. Now the genesis of these alleys must be long forgotten. The space occupied by them when I last saw it was largely covered by a school, the position of which seemed to me to have a peculiar fitness. Yet we cannot say the men who built the slums were sinners above the general population of Sunderland. Largely it was the result of circumstances and ignorance.

In early days Sunderland was but a small place at the mouth of the River Wear. A little further up the river was the large village of Bishopwearmouth. On the other side of the river was Monkwearmouth, the site of the great Abbey, which in Saxon days Benedict Biscop founded, and where he henceforth lived and worked. For generations Sunderland slumbered, the river mouth was used as a harbour, but was a poor one. In spite of that the coal trade grew, for Sunderland coal makes bright fires and burns slowly. In 1792 one hundred and ninety small ships sufficed for the coal exported from Sunderland, but in 1848 two thousand four hundred and ninety seven ships sailed from the Wear.

George Hudson, the Railway King, became Member for Sunderland 1848–59 and left his mark on the place, though I cannot remember ever hearing his name mentioned.

The port was so shallow that ships were obliged to load in the open roads, often to the great danger of the keel men, who brought the coal down the river in keels (lighters). George Hudson promoted the building of the South Dock, a great improvement. In the fifties and sixties the era of iron shipbuilding began and brought a new trade to Sunderland, where the riverside was soon lined with the staging for building new ships, and rang with the music of the hammer. The trade of Sunderland grew fast and the population increased in the same rate, but in the days before the workman's train, or of the horse tram or bus and the bicycle, the congestion of the population became extreme, for a workman must live within reasonable reach of his work. The population became congested and the fruit of this was the slums. 'Golden Alleys' were the natural product. About 1860 every available space was seized on for houses. Coronation Street and High Street, between which these particular slums lie, were, when I was there, the shopping streets of the district. Between them in the old days were the gardens of the tradesmen, who lived above their business premises. The price of land soared and very soon the gardens were sold as building sites and houses, with three floors and cobbled streets with a gutter down the middle, took the place of grass and flowers and shrubs. Men cared nothing then for fresh air and sunlight and sanitation in comparison with securing houses close to their work. Later with the advent of buses, trams and cheap railway fares, other sites at a distance became available and in these houses were generally found the very poor, the drinker and the criminal. Thus they degenerated into slums.

I had a neighbour in Sunderland from whom I learnt much. He was a doctor, who lived in the Borough Road—an able man, stirred by the district to a strong practical interest in housing. In 1895, the year in which I came to Sunderland, he produced an excellent little book, 'The Housing of the Working Classes' by Edward Bowmaker, M.D. I bought a copy and was absorbed in it. In a short plain way, reflected in its title, it placed before me what was England's greatest social need at the time. Around me the evil was great and the book pointed out a path to notable reforms.

At an early stage of my work in Sunderland I had collected a small class in the Institute for the study of social questions. We used to meet periodically in one of the cellars of the Institute for our discussions. Dr. Bowmaker's book on the 'Housing of the Working Classes' did me a great service in many ways, but not the least of those was that he brought before me the work of Miss Octavia Hill. The three cardinal features of her work that he stressed were:

'1. The acquisition of old and dilapidated property and its thorough repair.

2. Personal supervision and management.

3. The carrying out of the work on sound commercial principles.'

What was being more and more clearly seen every day was the great difficulty in dealing with the poorest classes—the unskilled labourers. Failing a scheme for reconstruction, Miss Octavia Hill of blessed memory, was of the opinion that much may be accomplished by the adaptation of existing premises. To this end she acquired possession of several blocks of buildings and either gradually or at once placed them in thorough repair. The strength of her scheme lay in the management.

My Men's Club were fired by it to try something ourselves. I proposed we should buy a house, put it in order and try as landlords to show what should be done in our slums. It was practicable and therefore an excellent idea. It was so easy to say what should be done, but what was needed was to show how to do it. This might be done by an experiment as landlords. The idea met with approval and there was no difficulty in acquiring a house for a modest sum. My fellow curate, Willy Paine, who was a man of means, put down most of the money. The house was in one of the alleys between

Coronation Street and High Street, the same as that into which I went when I was in the pursuit of Smith. The house was no worse than its neighbours, but we were quickly informed that our experiment could not succeed for the house was under a curse. A sailor had chucked a woman out of the top storey window one night and killed her, and the priest had laid a curse on it.

Dr. Bowmaker had given us an impressive list of the many serious affections of which structural and sanitary defects were the cause: chest diseases; bronchitis; consumption; rheumatism; follicular tonsillitis; diphtheria; croup; typhoid fever; erysipelas; diarrhoea; abscess; pyraemia; hospital gangrene; puerperal fever; pneumonia; headache; bilious attacks and various digestive ailments, sore throats and the like. Drink was both a 'cause and consequence of ill health'. So much for our prospects.

I think that all of my Social Studies class subscribed something, though I was careful to point out that it was not likely to be a paying proposition. Big subscriptions I did not expect, but we had manual help, which was of real value. We all did something to improve the house. Several of my Club helped to remove the building over the yard. Flintoff, one of the Men's Committee, who had been a slater, undertook to repair the roof. I was told off to act as his labourer, and to carry the slates up the ladder. We had to work at this for an hour before he went to work in the mornings. It meant very early rising, but I was never late.

The inside of the house was thoroughly cleaned and was soon resplendent with paint and whitewash. Our tenants, who were carefully chosen, seemed pleased. Very soon however there were serious complaints. We had put in a water closet that worked, and there was no other that worked in the near neighbourhood. Its fame spread and crowds gathered to enjoy its use. Unhappily it was a crowd not a queue, for the days of queues were not yet, and the people who rented this precious adjunct could never get near it. The trouble was baffling and an appeal to the police was of no use. They repudiated the task of regulating the approach of people to the W.C., laughed heartily and treated it as if it was a glorious jest.

Our experiment in housing caused us the usual trouble in collecting rents. A member of the Men's Club, who had had experience of its dangers, undertook the task. He stuck to it gallantly, although on one occasion when he had to make an entry through a window, he received a smart blow on the head, as he thrust his head in, from the lady of the house, who had armed herself with a piece of board.

The experiment was given up soon after I

left the parish and the house was sold. A small adverse balance on the account was discharged by Willy Paine, my fellow curate and most valued friend, with his usual generosity.

That was the last of my many unsuccessful efforts in Sunderland. More than three years had passed and I was nearing the end of my tether. My vicar transferred me to his own house, but what I wanted was a complete rest.

Sunderland made me a teetotaler. At Balliol there was not much drinking in my time, though there were one or two bad casualties. In my years in Sunderland the bitter cry of a poor woman of my acquaintance—'Oh, the drink! the weary, weary drink! We could all be happy if not for that,' lives always in my memory. I have been a teetotaler ever since my Sunderland experiences. A little later on in England, of course, the position was much improved by the legislation introduced by Mr. Lloyd George at the beginning of the First World War. To meet the crisis in the production of munitions produced by the higher wages being spent on alcohol, he raised the price of liquor, lowered the percentage of alcohol, and shortened the hours for which public houses were open. The measures produced a wonderful result, which held good though there are signs that some changes in the reverse direction in recent years are to be regretted. (This was written some years ago.)

There was one service to the community which I disliked doing exceedingly, though the law itself required it of me, and that was helping the police. I confess this to my shame. My weakness must not be conceived as indicating any want of respect for them. On the contrary I have great respect for them.

There would be an uproar at no great distance, and I would feel bound to go and see what is the matter. As I approach I see a crowd of women in full blast, booing and shouting. As I draw near and begin to push my way through the throng probably I see a policeman trying to bring along a drunken man. He is evidently finding the going difficult. When the constable catches sight of me, he may beckon for assistance, which the law and common justice require of me. The women are 'picking scoffs' at the constable, who is rather breathless. When I move forward to answer the appeal, there are cries from the women, 'Don't you help him, Mr. Barks, don't you help him. Let him leave the puir lad alone.' 'The puir lad' was probably a sad sinner, but these women generally had excuses for their men. I only once received a blow and that was unconsciously delivered. A young fellow was lying in the road roaring drunk. I beckoned to two or three neighbours standing by and said, 'Let us shove him into yonder yard or he will be getting into trouble.' They came to my help and I clutched at an arm, but he was too quick for me and landed me one on the chest. That was the only time I was ever struck and it was nothing. We soon had him safe out of the way of mischief.

One day an unexpected revelation dawned on me. Some errand took me into the old Parish of Sunderland, on which we bordered. Suddenly I realised that I was walking in a street called Nesham Street, and there was a Nesham Square hard by. The houses had not been unworthy in their day but were now very old property. I asked my mother, whose maiden name was Nesham, for the explanation of the mystery. Her answer made me realise that her family used to have connection with Sunderland and for a considerable time had been exporters of coal from the port and that one of my forbears at least had been married in the ancient parish church of Sunderland. The district, which so repelled me, had been, not the home, but the place of business, of my maternal ancestors. Their home was a few miles up river at Houghton le Spring and a source of wealth for three or four generations was the old Elizabeth Pit at Houghton, long since disused. Their connection with Sunderland made me feel uncomfortable.

Were they in any degree responsible for what I saw around me?

CHAPTER TWO

AUCKLAND AND SUNDERLAND

What of my spiritual development during my sojourn in Auckland and Sunderland? My year at Auckland meant much to me, for my inner life was quickened by my contact with my Bishop and with Cecil Bontflower, his chaplain. I went to Sunderland as one who was awaking spiritually and socially. Oxford had quickened me and Auckland deepened the process. Social questions also became real. Above the mantelpiece in Bishop Westcott's study hung the address presented to him after the great coal strike of 1892, when his intervention through a meeting held in Auckland Castle, had brought that bitter strike to a close. The memory of that day was vivid in the homes of the miners when I came North. While the meeting was in process, men from miles around had gathered in the Castle Drive, outside the garden railings, waiting hour after hour to hear the result. In their homes they were face to face with starvation. They had been given a sign by their agent by which to know at

35

once if the meeting were successful. He would wave his hand from a small window on the staircase leading to the front door. Suddenly the men saw the sign and knew that the days of starvation were at an end. A great shout went up. The crowd surged forward. The iron railings went down before them as they pressed forward to hear the proclamation of industrial peace and its terms proclaimed from the front door.

To Bishop Westcott this was the greatest triumph of his life and the men never forgot it. Above his mantelpiece in the study hung the address of thanks signed by both masters and men. At Auckland I learned the vital importance of great social questions.

In that year my inner life was quickened by my daily contact with the Bishop and Bontflower, his chaplain, but a book I read at this time also had a lasting effect. Some will think it a strange book to look back to with gratitude. It was Matthew Arnold's *Literature and Dogma*. I already knew something of his poems, and among them are some I read and reread. But at this time I came across his *Literature and Dogma*, which interested me deeply. It was, I think, just what I wanted at the moment. The book is disfigured by his mannerisms, but I found among less weighty matters, positive teaching in a clear and practical form.

He described the characteristics of the

teaching of Jesus as 'inwardness'. It pierces to the heart of man. There, is the true source of Conduct. 'Give me a clean heart, O God, and renew a right spirit within me.'

'The secret of Jesus is death to self and the rising to new life in Christ and God.'

What should be characteristic of Temper? Christ's life is the expression of Grace and Truth, to which Matthew Arnold applies the term 'Sweet Reasonableness', not a very attractive name but one to stimulate thought.

Matthew Arnold with all his faults was to me not only a teacher, but one who taught me to know Christ better. He disfigures his message, it is true, with flippancy and mannerisms.

Benjamin Jowett, who was an undergraduate with him at Balliol, said in after days that he was too flippant to be a prophet. He was flippant and his flippancy weakens his message, but in spite of it, there is, in a book like *Literature and Dogma* much positive teaching presented in a clear and practical form which was useful in its day.

At our meals in the Castle I often sat next to a Miss Prior, who had accompanied Mrs. Westcott from Cambridge, to help her with her many duties. She also had known Matthew Arnold well, but did not like him. 'He was so conceited.'

The Bishop from the first very definitely

attracted me, and Mrs. Westcott was kindness itself. Harry Westcott, the youngest of a long family, lived at home and served a curacy in Auckland. He was the soul of goodness but he had not the ability of the rest of the family. He could make fun like a clown and we often asked him for a performance—it was an extraordinary gift for a son of Bishop Westcott—whence did this gift descend on him? Mrs. Westcott certainly showed no signs of it. How interesting pedigrees will be when they can state in scientific form the characteristics of ancestors!

Of Cecil Bontflower I can only say that it would be difficult to conceive of anyone better fitted to fulfil the office which fell to him at Auckland.

My six fellow students were a good set. They were Aitken, afterwards vicar of Great Yarmouth which was for a time the most populous parish in England. I used to meet him later in convocation; Bolton, who died in his first curacy; Fyffe, who became Bishop of Rangoon; Parry, later Bishop of Guiana, and Ramsbotham, who preached at Charterhouse.

At first the social atmosphere was to me singularly strange and uncongenial, but later it no doubt helped very much. There was soon begotten in me a steadily deepening affection for my Bishop and a real sense of

Mrs. Westcott's kindness and goodness. By my fellow students I was soon called the heretic. Mrs. Westcott heard me thus addressed at lunch one day and intervened to say, 'Never mind their calling you that Mr. Bax. They used to call the Bishop a heretic when he was young.'

Mrs. Westcott was a dear old lady, but not perhaps so very old then after all, except in the estimation of youths of twenty two or thereabouts.

CHAPTER THREE

SOUTHWELL

From the slowly dimming memories of the foetid slums of Sunderland, I passed in the late autumn to a home near the castle in Nottingham—perhaps then and now the cleanest of England's great cities, as befitted the metropolis of the manufacture of lace. My work centred in an old country house, Thurgarton Priory, three miles from Southwell, nine from Nottingham. On a late November evening in 1898 I had my first talk with Dr. Ridding, first Bishop of Southwell, whose diocese, which then embraced both Nottinghamshire and Derbyshire, had been created in 1884.

Before that he had been Headmaster of Winchester and was perhaps the greatest Headmaster of his generation. He was accounted by Wykehamists almost as their second founder. He had spent something like £20,000 of his own money on the improvement of the school. In those days £20,000, carefully laid out, could effect something. The work included the turning of a stream into a new channel which thus made possible the construction of another cricket field.

After dinner we went into the drawing room, for a talk. The Bishop took his seat (which was rather a favourite one with him), on the broad padded top of a large brass fireguard and warmed himself, while I sat forward in an armchair and underwent 'my viva'. 'Who is your guide on social questions—is Canon Scott Holland?' he asked.

'Statistics,' I replied.

He looked surprised for a moment, and then objected, 'But they can be so misleading, and are so easily manipulated.' I agreed but urged that carefully gathered statistics are the nearest approach to a foundation of fact that we can get.

Whether he agreed, or not, I am not clear, but I passed my viva—whether or not with honours I do not know, and in due course I found myself spending a large part of my time at a kneehole table, dealing with letters and papers, or in his study, taking down his answers to letters in a sort of shorthand which I speedily developed for my own use.

For four years of my time, as his Domestic Chaplain and Secretary, I lived in Nottingham, and after that for two years in Southwell. My routine was to catch a train at 8.30 a.m. The journey took about fifteen minutes or a little more and I normally spent the time reading. One of the books I perused was Carlyle's *Frederick the Great*—a work, in the edition I possess, of ten volumes of approximately 300 pages each. I spent on it about 12 minutes a journey, if no one talked to me, and in due course of time reached the end of the ten volumes.

I did not know Dr. Ridding until he was approaching three score years and ten. He was then beginning to lose height, as his knees sagged a little and his shoulders began to show the weight of years, but his face was keen and beautiful. He was a Bishop of no recognised type, and his great value was a little obscured by the number of men of some special greatness, who filled that office in his day. He was not a great prince of the Church, like Benson; nor a historian, who marks an epoch, like Stubbs; nor a lesser light in the same craft like Creighton. He cannot be compared with Lightfoot in effective inspiration or in the enthusiasm

41

which he kindled in his Diocese; nor did he help to initiate a new movement for social reform, like Westcott; nor did he reinstate Christian doctrine like Gore in his early days. Nor was he a great ecclesiastic like Talbot. Yet in that fine scholarly face great qualities were reflected, for he represented the view of the thoughtful and instructed laity rather than that of the ecclesiastic. Like Gamaliel, he was ready to trust the power of truth, if it were given time to work. 'Trust truth' was one of his favourite maxims. The principles he stood for are at the root of all true progress. Bishops are seldom popular, but most people will admit that they have their uses. Few have been born to power. Dr. Ridding was too true an Englishman to care about what Carlyle had called 'Hebraic old clothes' nor did he desire to wear a mitre. He was a profound believer in the grace of God, but he held no advanced theories about it. His favourite text was, 'I will go forth in the strength of the Lord God,' and those words by the happy selection of Lady Laura Ridding, are graven on his tomb. His favourite words were 'real' and 'reality', which were used in a sense that had a deep ethical meaning akin to truth.

Geoffrey Benson, afterwards Lord Charnwood, one of his old boys, who had been a tutor at Balliol for a short time when I was up, used to pay an occasional visit to

Thurgarton. At his first visit after I became Chaplain he took me out for a walk in the garden to catechise me, as he was anxious to discover if I realised how great a man Dr. Ridding was. I gathered from Lady Laura that I satisfied my examiner.

Not a few clergy habitually crave for the guidance of authority of some sort; preferably that of the Church—failing that, of the Bishops or Convocation, and unhappily sometimes that of a Society. Ridding, like Westcott, would never make a man's mind up for him. He was ready to discuss and to open up new aspects of the problem, but the decision lay with the man himself. Only thus could the enquirer grow in mental and moral stature. 'Ridding distrusted system. Men, to come to their best, must develop naturally and learn to trust truth. Truth was the arbiter in all questions, not excluding those of faith. Insincerity and dishonesty of thought and action were repulsive to him. Party catchwords, secondhand opinions, professional mannerisms, imitated gestures, he could not away with.' (George Ridding, *Schoolmaster & Bishop*, p. 326)

While we talked, my eyes wandered round the room, the walls of which were hung with a number of water colour pictures the Bishop had collected in earlier days. I noticed among them the picture of a young woman.

Later on I was in the drawing room with one of the Miss Moberlys—I think the Miss Moberly who wrote the story of her strange experience at Versailles. I asked her who was the original of this rather striking picture. 'I do not know,' she answered, 'but I can guess the reason why it hangs there. It is extraordinarily like my sister, who was the Bishop's first wife.' The story of her death is recorded in 'Dulce Domum' written by her sister, Miss C. A. E. Moberly. It embodies a remarkable example of prevision. On June 24th 1859, Dr. Moberly, then Headmaster of Winchester and afterwards Bishop of Salisbury, recorded in Latin in his journal that while returning from a visit to a cottage where they spent holidays, with her son Arthur, Mrs. Moberly saw two men bearing a bier issued from a cottage called Potkiln. This was a hallucination. On July 18th, full three weeks after, on a delicious summer day, there was another expedition to the farm. Mrs. Ridding who was expecting a baby, was one of the party. She started for home earlier than the others. As they approached Potkiln, there was an accident and she was thrown out of the carriage. The expected child was born prematurely and mother and child died that evening. That was the great tragedy of Dr. Ridding's life. He had no child by his second marriage.

The spiritual road that Dr. Ridding

traversed was generally speaking like that along which I was trying to grope my way. 'We must be true to truth', 'Trust truth,' were the maxims by which he lived and which he always taught. His public life may be said to have begun with a sermon preached at St. Mary's, the University Church at Oxford, in 1864, shortly after he had been appointed Second Master of Winchester. It was on 'The Liberty of Teaching' and in defence of Benjamin Jowett, Master of Balliol, who was in trouble as a contributor to *Essays and Reviews*. The text of Dr. Ridding's sermon was Acts V 38, 39. 'Refrain from these men and let them alone, for if this Counsel or this work be of men, it will come to naught, but if it be of God, ye cannot overthrow it, lest haply ye be found even to fight against God.'

Another side of his character is illustrated by a small but revealing incident. He had had to wait an hour at a wayside station. How did you pass the time? asked Lady Laura on his return. 'I went out into the road, and found some collier lads playing marbles and I spent a pleasant hour in trying to show them how to play fair and without losing their tempers.'

It was at this time I first got to know Lady Waldegrave, Lady Laura's sister, of whom I was to see much when I became Rector of Radstock and for whom I had a great regard.

She was the second of the four daughters of the first Earl of Selborne, the Lord Chancellor. The second Earl of Selborne, who afterwards did such notable work in South Africa, came for a short visit from time to time, as did Lady Selborne, who was a daughter of Lord Salisbury, the Prime Minister of earlier years.

The Bishop never tried to overwhelm me by authority. I remember an occasion on which we had been discussing Old Testament criticism when he handed me his copy of Wellhausen, a great German Biblical scholar, and asked me to look at the pencil notes, which he had made on the margins of the pages. Again and again, he had convicted Wellhausen of inaccurate quotation. When I returned the volume to him he asked me what I thought of it. I said that it was indeed a warning not to take at face value what is put forward as evidence—even in the work of a famous scholar, but I still believed that in his general theory Wellhausen was substantially right. I have never known Dr. Ridding to try to overwhelm a man by authority, or resent a subordinate seeing truth differently to himself. My Bishop never became hard or fixed in his outlook.

Towards the end of my time at Thurgarton, Dr. Gore, now Bishop of Birmingham, brought one of his clergy to task for an article on the Virgin Birth. Bishop

Gore's summary treatment of Beebie shocked me, and I said in defence of Beebie to the Bishop, 'Well, at any rate he has acted very honourably in resigning.' 'I don't agree,' said the Bishop, 'He should have fought.'

My years as domestic chaplain were for me quiet and happy. It was just the sort of work I needed after Sunderland, and just the sort of leader. It gave me also a diocesan outlook from my contact with the work and life of the diocese.

I found the domestic staff at Thurgarton very friendly and helpful. From Howe, the head gardener, I learnt most of what I know of gardening. With Collins, the coachman, I always enjoyed a chat. These had been in his service at Winchester and went on with Lady Laura Ridding to Wonston after the Bishop's death. Heath, the butler, was a breeder of prize winning Buff Orpington fowls at a time when they were the fancy. From him I had my first lessons about fowls. I always remember one of his remarks. We were expecting the Rural Deans for their Annual Meeting. I went into the dining room to see that all was right. There was a slight difficulty about seating. Can't they sit a bit nearer to each other? I ventured to remark. 'No Sir,' he replied, 'You see, Rural Deans sit rather big.' Perhaps in the lean days to follow of the war and after my suggestions could have been adopted.

CHAPTER FOUR

THURGARTON AND SOUTHWELL

Thurgarton Priory had a long history. From the corner, where my desk stood in the library, I looked out upon the garden. Over against the church were some tall cherry trees which in their season were snowlike with blossom. A staircase led from the library down into the ancient church of Thurgarton, once the church of the priory. The modern house adjoining it was built over the ancient crypt of the priory, whose prior in the Middle Ages was the chief ecclesiastic in the County of Nottingham.

To me its undying interest lies in the fact that it had been the home of Walter Hilton, the author of *Scala Perfectionis* (*The Ladder of Perfection*). He died in 1396. His book was printed by Wylkyn de Worde in 1494. It and kindred works by other writers have opened up for us a little known aspect of religious life in the Middle Ages.

I do not remember that the Bishop ever spoke of Walter Hilton to me, though Lady Laura Ridding made me acquainted with his name, but not with his book. Yet that book had greatly influenced many of the finest minds and characters of his own day and for three or four generations after. It was not until many years later that I stood with my back against one of the great Norman pillars in the church, remembering that Walter Hilton may have often stood upon this very spot. A stone figure of Christ found not many years ago in a rockery in the priory garden and now restored to the church may have held his reverent gaze in days long past. Through the shallow green valley, where the priory stands, he must often have walked and may at times have taken shelter from the sun and rain under the shade of some oak that still survives.

He had learned to tap a deep source of power, which so many neglect, 'To me there was spoken a secret word and the veins of his whispering mine ear hath perceived. The inspiration of Jesus is a hidden word, for it is privily hid from all lovers of the world and shown to His lovers ... for every gracious knowing of truth, felt with inward favour and spiritual delight, is a privy whispering of Jesus in the ear of a clean soul.'

The typical mystical experience, Dean Inge tells us, is just prayer, 'Anyone who has really prayed and felt that his prayers are heard, knows what mysticism is.' The rungs of the ladder of perfection are purification, illumination, union.

There was, I think, a community of mind in some ways between my dear old Bishop and the medieval mystic. Who can doubt that the writer of 'the Litany of Remembrance' also knew the Way of Purification and that it led to Illumination. Of the third rung, Union, who will dare to speak? Yet as Dean Inge reminds us, 'We must beware of regarding Union as anything more than an infinite process, though at its end it is part of the eternal counsel of God. There is a sense in which it is already a fact and not merely a thing desired.'

My old Bishop was a strong believer in the intense interest and usefulness of the life of a parish clergyman, 'If only men threw themselves into their work! They really dealt with life.' In his opinion the calling of a clergyman offers a readier and perhaps an easier road to effective usefulness than any other career. I believe that he was right.

To my Bishop, I am sure, all true Christians were of the same church and the walls of partition which are so often the narrowness, the prejudices, the traditions of men, should be thrown down.

On June 17th 1899 I was married by the Bishop to Diana, daughter of Colonel Edward Napier (of the Ettrick family) and Mrs. Napier. We went to Holland for our honeymoon. There is good reason to believe that a part of our family long long ago came from Holland, and for a joke we agreed to ask the first likely person we met in the train in Holland if he had ever come across the name Bax. His reply was, 'Yes. My best friend is called Bax.' I received my first dressing down from my wife on my wedding day. England were playing Australia at the time of our wedding and while we waited for our train to start from Liverpool Street, I bought a paper to see what the score was. My wife regarded this as highly improper. I ought not to think of such things on my wedding day.

Less than eighteen months before I had fallen in love with my wife, and now I fell in love with matrimony. We set up house in 10 Regent Street, Nottingham. My life was practically that of a business man. I left home every day except Sunday in time to reach Thurgarton for 9 a.m. breakfast and returned when my work was done, normally at 4.30 p.m. Sometimes of course I stayed on for dinner.

In the summer on Saturdays I played cricket for the village team. The bowling was good, but the batting poor as a rule, as was the case generally with village teams. At this time my cricket was greatly improved.

Among our chief friends in Nottingham were a Dr. and Mrs. Laws. The former was a leading oculist there. One day I casually imparted to him the information that my sight had never been tested since it was first tested by Crickett (a well known oculist of the previous generation) when I was eight years old, and my glasses were still of the strength he prescribed at that time. 'Then I advise you to come to me at once and let me have a look at them,' he said. I did as he advised and shortly after received my new spectacles.

That evening we were going to a meeting, and I put them on for the first time as we sat in the hall. As we came out into the clear night I stood transfixed upon the steps and exclaimed aloud—'Good Heavens! What has happened to the sky?' Where I had seen ten stars before, I now saw hundreds. I had lost a lot by the omission to see an oculist periodically. In cricket my bowling had not been bad at school. My opposite number bowled for Sandhurst in the next season and my average was very little below his in our last term at school together. As a batsman, although I could stonewall with some success, I could never see to hit, and have never been able to do so. Then it must also be remembered that I have never had a lesson from a professional. Bowling was hardly wanted from me by the village team as several could bowl, but I became very useful to them as a bat. No doubt the change of glasses greatly helped my batting. I enjoyed this village cricket very much. They were a nice set of fellows. I had a glorious remark made to me by our umpire, a farmer. 'Mr.

Bax,' he said as we walked home from a match, with a team whose umpire was under suspicion. 'I always try to do what's fair, but if I see the other umpire trying to do a thing or two, I always try to make it fair.' We had won in spite of the other team's umpire.

On June 21st 1900 I was writing at my desk in the library at Thurgarton about 10 a.m. when a telegram was handed to me. It read, 'Come home at once, Marshall.' Dr. Marshall was our much loved doctor; I hurried up from the station at Nottingham full of foreboding. The doctor was there when I arrived, and he drew me into the drawing room, and looking grave, explained either that something had gone wrong, or it was twins. Such a possibility as twins had never crossed my mind, nor had I ever realised how prolonged and anxious confinement may be. It was June 21st—in any case the longest day of the year, and to me every hour was two or three times as long as it should be. I could not read. Lunch or tea seemed repulsive. There was no one to talk to, and for view there was only the house similar to ours across the road. At length the sun sank and the lengthening shadows foretold the night. Suddenly there was the wailing cry of a small baby and after an interval that of another. It was twins— Stephen, now the father of three sons, and Clemency, the mother of my only granddaughter, had been born into the world. What a business it was! There was only one cradle, and one lot of clothes, and the mother had only one pair of hands. Neighbours were very kind. Within an hour another cradle had arrived and a bundle of clothes. My wife found many good friends in Nottingham. Mr. A. L. Rowse had written much of the interest and the beauty of the city. We could have told much of the kind hearts there. That is the story of the birth of Stephen and Clemency. Thrice more a child was born to us and each time to ordinary anxieties was added the fear that it might again be twins, or even triplets. Few know how much it adds to the anxieties of childbirth if on the first occasion it is twins.

One of my most interesting interviews in Nottingham was with John Burns, who had taken a leading part in the Dock Strike and had intervened to help the dockers for the sake of working class solidarity, although he was himself an engineer. In time he passed up from being a strike leader to being the president of the local government board. He came to Nottingham to address a Temperance Meeting and I was invited to meet him. He had been described as a man of fantastic vanity, but I found him very likeable. When my allotted ten minutes had elapsed, Mr. Jesse Boot was announced and I rose to go. 'No, sit down,' he said, 'I should like you to be present,' and turning from me he welcomed Mr. Jesse Boot. 'How many shops have you, Mr. Boot?' 'I have forty now,' was the reply. 'Your hair is very white, Mr. Boot. How old are you?' 'Perhaps if you only had one shop, your hair would not have been so white.' And so on, but Mr. Jesse Boot answered most good humouredly and the tone of the conversation changed, and the 'Goodbye' was most cordial on both sides.

Anxieties came with parenthood, yet on the whole we faced them with light hearts.

A friend wrote of her visit to us at Nottingham, 'I spent a very happy fortnight with them in November 1900. Arthur and Diana made me feel quite old, they were so terribly young and frolicsome. He used to tip her over backwards in her chair at dinner if he disapproved of her words, and leave her there until he saw fit to haul her up.'

I have never forgotten, nor ever shall, the happenings at one visit we paid where we witnessed a memorable scene. It was at the house of a very rich and successful man. He was a widower and his home was looked after by an unmarried daughter. As we sat at tea, the eyes of the daughter became fixed on a spot on the floor. As she finished what she was saying, she rose and pulled the bell. The butler appeared. She pointed at the spot on the floor, and said, 'Remove that insect.' It was a spider. The butler said, 'Very good, madam,' and bowed. In a few minutes he returned, followed by two footmen, one of whom bore a dustpan and the other a brush. The butler pointed majestically at the spider. The foremost footman knelt and held the dustpan in front of it. The second footman knelt and brushed it into the pan. Then they rose and the procession was reformed and in the same order as that in which they had entered they disappeared, carrying the offending insect with them. Of its fate I know nothing.

I wonder what the feelings of the footmen were, and whether they were pillars of the constitution. I wonder too what was the future history of the poor spider. Did it come to a horrid end? Did they put it out of the window to continue its useful service of catching flies?

We then moved to Southwell and took up residence in the Old Palace.

The Old Palace was the remains of what had been the southern residence of the Archbishop of York. Its garden wall was formed by the somewhat ruined outer wall of the old quadrangle, and twenty yards or so to the north side stands one of the most beautiful of the smaller cathedrals of England. The Old Palace has been a ruin ever since the days of Cromwell, but a fragment of it, with the great hall, has been restored. We had two big bedrooms and a small one. Besides an entry from the back stairs, a big stone staircase led upstairs from the front door and terminated in our bedroom. Naturally, any unguided party walked up the front staircase, and then appeared in our bedroom. On one occasion we encountered a ducal party there. Happily as they also had a sense of humour, I think they enjoyed their visit.

The great front door opened on to a wide corridor, which terminated in the kitchen. Down that corridor the cathedral bells echoed and reverberated. The drawing room and dining room were of great size and the kitchen and its offices baronial. The drawing room was papered with a wonderful Chinese paper, which had been placed there by a former resident, who had made a fortune in China in earlier days as a ship's captain. Our furniture was a nothing in these splendid apartments.

Our new home was full of romance. Given a full moon behind the ruins of an historic building, and it is hard to avoid dreaming. We had at Southwell material to inspire visions. Cardinal Wolsey who was also Archbishop of York, spent some weeks at the end of his life in the Old Palace. Cavendish, the Secretary of the Cardinal Archbishop, has left an account of those long past days, which conjures up its forgotten happenings, some of which our imagination can reproduce. The first floor of the East wall may have been the scene of the visit of the King's Messengers of recall to London, to the Archbishop. They came when it was already dark, and a fireplace with a beautiful carved mantelpiece and the gap left by a fallen oriel window in the East wall, may well mark the room where they were received by Wolsey.

The great Cardinal was spending his last summer here in disgrace and retirement, enjoying himself more creditably in the days of adversity than in those of prosperity, for he composed many grievous and long standing quarrels among the neighbouring gentry, and reconciled husbands and wives. For these months at least he was God's diplomatist rather than the King's.

'Late on the eve of Corpus Christi, when the inmates of the palace had retired to rest, the messengers arrived from the Court. Wolsey came to them in his private dining chamber in his night apparel, and on learning that they desired to talk with him apart, he drew them aside into the recess of the great window, and there talked with them secretly. After long communication they lifted out of a mail a certain coffer covered with green velvet and bound with bars of silver and gilt, from which they took an instrument having many great seals

58

hanging at it, whereunto they put more wax for my lord's seal; and then, none else save the porter, knowing of their visit they departed to the Earl of Shrewsbury's, because they would be there or ever he stirred in the morning.

'The despoiled minister gave them each four gold sovereigns of gold as they left, saying that if he had been of greater ability, their reward should have been better. After they were departed they were not contented with their reward: Howbeit if they knew what little store of money he had at that time they would have given him hearty thanks; but nothing is more lost or castaway than is such things, which may be given to such ingrate persons.' This happened more than four hundred years ago, nor was this the only tragic association of the Old Palace at Southwell.

We loved the house, but our entrance was inauspicious. The maids had been sent on in advance. It was November and it was twilight when they arrived. Their approach was through the Churchyard, where interments had been made right up to the palace wall. They had entered through the great door, which ominously clanged behind them. The only light was the splendid kitchen fire at the end of the corridor. They reached it and collapsed by the fire on the floor. Never before had they been in such a

59

place. Stalwart Anna, our nurse from Brunswick, with piteous cries invoked the Fatherland, the others hid their faces in the mattresses, airing by the fire, and sobbed aloud. When we arrived a little later, they lay there in a bunch lamenting loudly, and did not stir until we in despair had begun to prepare our beds.

Our home was a strange but fascinating one. The back staircase met the corridor just before the baronial kitchen. The main staircase also had a door which gave admission to the great hall, which was loved by our children. It was a delightful place for a children's party. All that was needed was a big blazing fire, easily provided then, which afforded light as well as heat, and a few chairs to seat adults. In our experience our children's guests never desired games. Their only wish was to be left to join hands and race up and down the great room. The parents sat grouped in front of the fire and talked, while from their pictures on the walls past canons of Southwell looked down benignly on the racing children. These parties were a great success.

In the night there were sometimes noises the origin of which we could never fathom. If I have been downstairs once, I have been downstairs twenty times or more to investigate what was happening. Sometimes we were awakened by a noise as though all the chairs in the baronial kitchen were being pushed across the stone floor; at another the great outer door would slam with an echo that reverberated up and down the stone corridor and through the house. I would leap out of bed and hurry down below, where all was by then still as the grave. Every chair was in position in the kitchen and the great door was as firmly locked and bolted with the key in the lock as we had left it when we went up to bed.

It was the only experience I have ever had of a poltergeist or 'A spirit that makes itself known by noises' (to use the description the dictionary provides), if that was the cause. We could make nothing of it. The children used to describe from time to time a man in a close fitting green dress who would enter the bedroom, where they were put to rest in the afternoon, by the great staircase, and walk across the room to the door which led to the other staircase. As he crossed the room he would be silhouetted against the window. They were never frightened by the vision and would mention it as a piece of news. Had it not been for the noises, which on a number of occasions sent me to explore the house, one would not have paid any attention to the children's stories. I never saw anything myself, nor did my wife, but we were both awakened on many occasions over a brief period by the noises downstairs to which I have referred, and I confess that I very much disliked running downstairs to explore, but always did.

After a time the nuisance ceased. If someone desired to frighten us out of the Old Palace, I suppose that he had despaired of success, and he realised that his method of effecting his purpose led nowhere and had its dangers.

Our old family servant, Smithie, declared that someone had entered her room on more than one occasion, but she never shouted for us though we were only two doors away. So far as I know no one else ever had the same experience.

After we left the Old Palace was enlarged and changed in many respects. Southwell when we lived there was an embodiment of the spirit of 'Cranford'. The Rector, Canon Trebeck, an old Christ Church man, was a fine upstanding figure, who had in his day been a notable lightweight boxer, but had long lost his qualification for that class. His wife was a daughter of John Wordsworth, sometime Bishop of Salisbury, a very gracious figure. But Southwell was very conventional, very old world, but very kind. A happening, while we were there, illustrates its likeness. When Canon Trebeck died, a clergyman was sent to take charge temporarily of the parish. He had in him not a little of the spirit of St. Francis, and, as would probably have been the case if St. Francis himself had appeared at Southwell, he provoked much criticism. He had a mind above finance and organisation, but had been known literally to bestow upon a beggar a garment taken on the spot from his own body, as he stood halted in the street.

It fell out that he scandalized two dear old ladies and their report to me was as follows:

'What a terrible person that is that the Bishop has sent here to help!'

'What has he done?' I replied, 'He is a really very good fellow.'

'We don't like him anyway. What do you think we saw him doing yesterday afternoon when we were taking our walk?'

'Well what was it?'

'I saw him positively saying his prayers in a field!'

But we must not misjudge them. These ladies were really full of the milk of human kindness, though in the bondage of convention.

The day came when we, Diana and I, had our first quarrel with each other. I have no idea what it was all about, but it was very bitter. A breach in our happy life had been opened, which perhaps could never be repaired. Not knowing what to do, I left the Old Palace and turned slowly and thoughtfully to my right, past the south porch of the cathedral and around the chancel. In front of me was the glorious chapter house. Of its beauty I saw nothing. What did I care for crotchets or finials or even the massive buttresses which blocked my vision when my happiness had been wrecked—perhaps for ever. As I rounded the last buttress I halted like a man turned to stone. A few feet away from me was Diana. For three seconds we were speechless and then her face said—'Aren't you going to give me a kiss and say "sorry".' I, weakly, obeyed. I was quite incapable of looking fiercely at her, instead we both burst out laughing, and returned to the Old Palace hand in hand.

What a wonderful meeting that was and how unexpected! Was it a special providence? I have my own theory as to how it happened, but happily was too wise to raise the question, but I do not think that it was a special providence. I have always held that women have very good wits, when they choose to use them, and that they always expect the men to make the first advance when they have a difference with their husband, but they are quite ready to make it easy for the sinning husband to repent, confess and be shriven.

The last Christmas came on which the Bishop according to his custom celebrated in the cathedral. Lady Laura says in a little memoir of Diana which she wrote, 'After the service we went into the Old Palace where the Revd. A. N. Bax, his chaplain, lived. Then came a moment which will always be painted on my memory as a beautiful picture. Round the Bishop came a group, dewy with youth and loveliness. A tiny kid and a puppy, devoted friends, a kitten also allowed to join in the frolic; a crawling baby and the Bishop's special allies—Stephen and Clemency Bax, three year old twins. The bounding kid with its budding horns, the solemn lurching puppy, the infants and the two goats browsing around the old ruins, which framed the group, made the composition, such as Poussin would have sketched in his foreground. The Bishop weighted with seventy years, but with his young eyes and wonderful smile, made a harmonious contrast, as beautiful as that seen yearly on his terrace at Thurgarton, where every spring, the great wild cherry trees were decked in a snowy glory of blossom which shone in perfect union with the tulips squills and hypaticas at their feet. The Bax babies were devoted to the Bishop and used to send him frequent offerings of toys and paper boats "to swim in his bath".' When told that God had taken him Home, at his death, little Stephen said sadly, 'He was a welly great friend of mine'.

That Dr. Ridding did not grow old with years is illustrated by a clause in his Litany of

Remembrance, 'In times of doubts and questionings, when our belief is perplexed by new learning and teaching, when our faith is strained by Creeds, by doctrines, by mysteries beyond our understanding, give us the faithfulness of learners and the courage of believers in Thee; give us boldness to examine and faith to trust all truth; patience and insight to master difficulties, stability to hold fast our tradition with enlightened interpretation, to admit all fresh truth made known to us, and in times of trouble to grasp new knowledge readily and to combine it loyally and honestly with the old; alike from stubborn rejection of new revelations, and from hasty assurance that we are wiser than our fathers, Save us and help us we humbly beseech Thee, O Lord.'

On August 30th 1904 the Bishop died. In spite of a great sorrow his had been a happy life. In these last days he said more than once, 'I should like to live my life over again.' In these days when we hear so much talk of 'Frustration' and pessimism and futility, it is delightful to remember the happy way in which as strength ebbed rapidly, he viewed life.

The weeks after his death were for me a period of great and perhaps unreasonable anxiety. I had a wife and three children to provide for, for Oliver was born in 1902. I had been ten years in Orders, and was no longer fitted for a curacy, but where was the living to come from, now that the Bishop was dead? I had also a special reason for anxiety. Shortly after the Bishop's death I was asked as a member of the Churchmen's Union if I would sign 'A Declaration on Biblical Criticism' which it was proposed to issue. The Declaration would today attract little attention as Christian opinion in England at any rate has accepted the points then at issue. It pointed out that as many of the clergy had already, with advantage to the Christian Faith, welcomed the results of Old Testament criticisms, they might now receive authorative encouragement to face the critical problems of the New Testament. It ended with an expression of confidence that the 'Faith of the Church in years to come, whatever historical revisions may await us, will stand without risk and without discontinuity, upon the spiritual foundations to which Christian experience and the Creed of the Church alike bear testimony.'

I read it with complete sympathy.

I handed the letter to my wife, and said, 'Read this and tell me what in your view I ought to do.' Her reply was prompt and what I expected. 'This is what you believe, and you have no choice.' Strange as it may seem to people today, the issue of this Declaration provoked quite a storm in the press. Only two clergy of the Southwell

67

diocese were among those who signed the original letter of invitation, of whom one was my old vicar, R. T. Talbot, now Vicar of St. Werburgh's, Derby, and the other myself.

I was among the hundred clergy who issued the Declaration and when it was circulated I alone simply appeared as M. A. Oxon, for my Bishop was dead, and I was waiting for something to turn up.

The announcement of the name of the new Bishop of Southwell was not reassuring.

My Bishop's successor was naturally anxious to have a chaplain of his own selection, and in any case it was quite time for me to return to parish work. I went as far as to consult a friend who had gone to Canada, about going to clerical work out there. Just as I was preparing with my wife, babies and all, for a leap in the dark, the solution to my problems appeared.

I received a letter from my old college, Balliol, offering me the living of Duloe, a parish lying between Liskeard and Looe in Cornwall.

We visited it at once and left the Midlands in a thick Trent Valley fog. We spent the next day at Duloe in beautiful winter sunshine, which is not uncommon in Cornwall. We ate a most attractive midday meal, which had been prepared for us by the ex-cook, who lived in the village, and as we ate we looked out upon the lawn and lime avenues bathed in sunshine. We fell in love with the rectory straight away. House and garden and the country around alike are beautiful. We returned to Southwell, rejoicing in our lot.

Very soon the day for our departure came. We broke the journey at Bristol and we milked Phyllis, our nanny goat, in a waiting room there, before we went to our hotel. She was tame enough to follow a trap or a ridden horse like a dog. She drew a little wicker cart in harness like a pony—in which the twins sat instead of the pram which was now used for Oliver. On Dartmoor she would accompany us on an expedition and be milked at our destination to provide us with milk for our tea. She was always a little tiresome about standing, so one of us would hold her up by the back legs, while the other milked her.

The milking at the station attracted a good deal of adverse attraction and one outraged and prudish old lady went off to fetch the station master to stop such goings on in public. On arrival he addressed Diana: 'Madam. I should be only too glad to put my private office at your service' and we swept out headed by the station master. Many years later, when Clemency was staying at Mrs. Eden's house at Kingston near Taunton, a lady at a dinner party described how she had seen a mother bring a goat into the waiting room and start milking it for her small children and how many of the occupants were outraged. Clemency revealed that she was one of the children waiting for Phyllis's milk which caused much merriment. Phyllis lived for many years after this as a pensioner and family pet.

CHAPTER FIVE

DULOE

We had bade farewell on February 24th 1905 and stayed for a few days with my mother at Devonport and on March 3rd, Diana's thirtieth birthday, I was inducted into the Rectory of Duloe by the Ven. H. H. du Boulay, Archdeacon of Bodmin.

My predecessor, Canon Paul Bush, was a clergyman of the Squire type, of strong conventional outlook, and a moderate High Churchman, who for fifty years (1850–1904) maintained an armed neutrality with dissenters and liberals. He was much respected and in some degree popular, but was too much of an autocrat for general acceptance. In his old age, I was told, he had deepened spiritually, and mellowed considerably. My informant ascribed the development to the effect on him of a mission he had caused to be held in his parish. As regards their new rector a farmer was reported to have said, 'Us don't care what un preaches. He's first got to prove himself a man.'

We had our own ideas and chosen way of life, which meant for the parish a considerable break with the past. A great friend of my wife, whom she had known all her life, and who was substantially older, wrote thus of our early days. 'I went to Duloe nearly every spring during their time there and have happy recollections of my visits. The place was very pretty but not bracing. It was Arthur's first living and it was prophecied that Diana would make the place sit up and truly she did. Having been accustomed for fifty four years to one of the old fashioned type of parsons, the people found the changed ways in general, and the parson's wife in particular, a decided puzzle. Had they but understood they would have known that though she was out of the common, yet in her they had the trust of friends—one in a thousand. But her unaccountable originality was what they found hard to swallow and it was long before she made real headway with the people. Cornish folk are dour at the best of times. Duloe was so out of the world, that ways common and everyday in other places were quite unknown there. So when the very

71

modern parson and parsoness by example and precept tried to start a new order of things, it proved rather upsetting. They had to gain their experience, and Diana, not unnaturally, resented the hasty judgement meted out to them.'

'Remember, that the friendly man makes friends.'

At a very early period of my life as Rector those words were said to me by an old farmer. I needed them and they stuck by me, and how true they are! I hope that they are taught in our theological colleges. At any rate I have found great friendliness in my parishes. It is nearly fifty years since I went to Duloe, and there were a number of people there to whose memory I look back with gratitude, and affection even now. There were my churchwardens, Mr. Clogg, whose life had been saddened by an accident. His little daughter, then a small child, was behind a door which he opened suddenly. The key struck her in the eye, and destroyed the sight. There was Mr. Philip Brown, already in those early days a scientific farmer, and a most careful accountant. On one occasion he was called on to show his accounts in Court, and the judge commended him highly for the way in which they were kept, as he handed him back his account book. I used from time to time to accompany him in his walk around his farm, and from him picked up something about cows, and how to distinguish and know the value of different grasses and a variety of other useful knowledge. When, with the co-operation of the schoolmaster, I asked some farmers to bring a cow or horse to the school and to tell our country children about them, their breeds and methods of handling them, food, sicknesses, cleanliness etc. he at once volunteered and he was the first to come.

There was Bennet Toms, who gave up the sea to return home to look after his old father and the farm. He was a fine type of Christian, whose religion beautified his life. His cousin, Elizabeth Jamblin, the daughter of another farmer, came to look after the old man and the house and to our great pleasure in course of time, she and Bennet were married.

The villagers did not average the same high type as the farmers but the cause was quite obvious, and was shown by the statistics of population. In 1871 the return for Duloe was 1109 and by 1901 it had dropped to 735, or without Herodsfoot to about 550. During that period the most stirring and enterprising of the young men in many a Cornish village went away to South Africa or America, and when he was settled, sent for his girl to come out to him. It was not often that they returned to Cornwall,

73

though we had two or three instances of it. It was said that when Uncle Jack (the Cornishman) got into a nice job he began to use his shoulders to dislodge the man next to him, and then sent for a nephew to take his place, but probably that was an exaggeration. At any rate the village life suffered much from emigration and also from the natural attraction of the Navy. The pick of the young men went and seldom returned. Sometimes, for one cause or another, their intention was kept secret. A landowner further north told me an amusing instance of this. He had some good fishing on his estate. One day his keeper to his surprise found a young fellow from the parish fishing their best stretch of water. He warned him that he would hear more of this. The fisherman put up his rod and went quietly away. The next day, to the astonishment of the keeper, history repeated itself. On the third day following, there he was again. The keeper was dumbfounded. When the summons was issued a day or two later, it could not be served, for the bearer found that the fisherman had left for America. He had secured all the fishing he could before he went and no one except his mother had known of his imminent departure.

The oldest of the inhabitants of the parish were John Broad, who was born in 1809 and was aged 96 when we came to Duloe, and his second wife who was a little younger than he. Their honeymoon was strangely kept. After they were married they walked to Bodmin nearly twenty miles away 'to see a gentleman hanged'. If it suffices for an experience to be unforgettable to make it desirable, they had attained it. There were then still one hundred crimes punishable by death, although shop-lifting to the value of five shillings, or blackening the face in commission of a theft by night, or for a notorious thief to reside in Northumberland or Cumberland, or to injure Westminster Bridge, had been removed from the number of Capital Crimes; but for what this victim suffered I do not recollect, nor whether he belonged to the 'County'. At any rate the remembrance of the scene remained with John Broad and his wife through their long lives, and cheered the slowly passing hours of old age.

Poor old Southern was another 'bed lier', for that was the common designature of the category to which John Broad and he belonged. He was tended by his devoted daughter, Mary. My wife took a special fancy to the old gentleman and discovered that he loved a beef steak pudding. Then on some festival—I think a birthday—she made one and took it to him as a surprise. When she came again, as no reference was made to it, she said, 'Did you enjoy the beef steak pudding?' The reply was unexpected. 'I never had such a disappointment in my life, never!' 'What was the matter?' 'I was that looking forward to it, and I said to Mary, "Mind you bring me some of that pudding for my dinner", I put some in my mouth and had to spit it out again. There was onion in it. I cannot abide onions.'

Mr. William Hocken, senior, was a retired farmer, and the leading supporter of the Chapel. We conceived at our first meeting a mutual liking for each other, and his son, who had succeeded his father in the farm, was like myself, a member of the cricket team. On Christmas Days and Good Fridays the Hocken family and most of their congregation would be in their proper place in church. On my last Sunday the chapel was closed, and their congregation came in a body. When I told the old man that I was leaving, he broke down, and when I tried to comfort him, he said, 'With you at the rectory there has been five years of peace.'

Mr. Nutcher had been in the Navy, which he entered as a boy, and had risen to the rank of lieutenant (in those days a remarkable achievement) by long and valuable service. He had married a charming wife and had settled at Duloe, where his sister-in-law was the wife of the schoolmaster. It was always a pleasure to me to meet him, except on one occasion, when I found him carrying his gun and plunged in woe. The tears were streaming down his face. 'Whatever is the matter?' I asked. 'I have been out after a rabbit,' he replied 'and I have shot my dear dear dog!'

There is another old man whom I must also recall to memory, for he gave me one of the great pleasures of my life. He was old, perhaps prematurely, crippled and walking slowly with the aid of two sticks. He wore an old felt hat pressed down above his round face and he earned a poor living by breaking stones. I met him frequently and if I did not show signs of stopping, he would stop me with a request to know the time. Sometimes I would sit down by him and try to crack stones. I could never achieve the knack, and my want of success was to him a source of great pleasure. If I had the governess cart with me and the evening was drawing on, I would offer him a lift home, which he was always glad to have, for his progress on his legs and two sticks was very slow. To get him up to the only possible position—a seat on the tail board—was very difficult. Briony, my mare, was always anxious to get on, and I had to control her with one hand and assist him with the other. He was heavy and up went the shafts when he seated himself. As soon as he was secure I had to find my way in as best I could for she was all eagerness to start.

I shall leave Bill Tamblin now, but I will tell the sequel of our friendship later—a source of deep and lasting pleasure to me. I never got to know much of his history. He only once entered the church in my time, and the public house was undoubtedly more in his line.

Briony, a strong cob, was a good little mare, but she had her tricks. She was always anxious to ration a ride. When I had gone what she judged to be a suitable distance, she would begin to shy at every conceivable object, but she never got me off. I knew her little ways. When I was visiting a house no hitch, that I could procure, would hold her while I was paying my visit. She would pull the metal straight with strong jerks. As she never ran away and there were no motors then, and very little traffic, I took to leaving her unfastened, a practice which never miscarried. She spent her time feeding in the hedge. She was very good with the children. I have seen our children playing 'Follow my leader' under her belly, and she with her neck bent around, quietly watching their game, which she seemed to enjoy.

We were very good friends and certainly on two occasions she behaved admirably. On one of these a rein broke when we were travelling fairly fast. She knew her way and took a corner correctly, but it was a tense moment. If she had cut the corner, the

78

family would have been spilled in the road. The other occasion was in Liskeard on the day of the local Agricultural Show. I was in the cart with my two elder children. We heard a shouting and a moment after there came into view a brake drawn by two runaway horses. The driver had hold of the reins and was running with them trying to keep them on their own proper side of the road. I drew in right against the stone wall on our side of the road and told the children to sit in the bottom of the cart. The brake passed without a collision, but it was a matter of inches for the horses were pulling strongly across the road. Briony's conduct was admirable, and so was the children's.

Duloe was a very hilly parish and some of the hillsides were covered with oak scrum, which at that time was in place still cut and burnt for charcoal, which was exported to the north country steelworks. The bark was stripped and used for tanning. Once in a way I came across the woodmen at work and took the opportunity to improve acquaintance.

From the first at Duloe we were faced with a great difficulty. Our means were inadequate and something had to be done to make them sufficient. To the uninitiated the statement about the income in Crockford at first sight suggested that the income was ample. For 1903 the return of income was as follows: 'Gross income T.R.C. (tithe rent

79

charge) £616. 45 acres of Glebe. Gross income £506, net £258.'

The explanation of the difference between real and nominal value was as follows. The income was mostly from tithe and tithe varied with the price of corn and the price of corn at the date was very low. Upon the gross income from tithe rates were then charged and rates were mounting. This was in spite of the fact that tithe was 'earned income'. Later this was altered. There was also the charge of £50 a year, rate free for Herodsfoot, a small parish cut out of Duloe, which had to be paid out of the Duloe income. Hence the reduction of the gross income from £506 a year to £258 net.

The Rectory house and the stable and farm buildings were more suitable for a small squire than for a clergyman, but two fields were happily in hand and we had a big garden, in which we could grow far more than vegetables for the house. We were young and hopeful and were prepared to face our difficulties in our own way.

Our first shock was dilapidations, a very sore one. As presented by the surveyor, and accepted, they were not immoderate but when begun, the village carpenter reported to us that there had been a mistake by the surveyor, and the cost of it would fall on us. There was a crack in the plaster of our bedroom wall, apparently a trivial matter, and calculated as such, but when examined by the workmen, was found to be very serious. The walls of the old part of the house were of cob, and in an extension to the house a passage had been made in one wall lengthways with an arched roof. That held all right, but a drawing room wall had been pierced for the construction of the bow window and the wall over the hole had never been supported by an arch or in any other way. The crack was a sign that the arch was giving, and the wall was likely soon to fall and would carry part of the roof with it. Now the roof must be supported with timber and the wall rebuilt, and the charge would fall on us.

Our first personal problem at Duloe was to balance income and expenditure. This was a more practical proposition than it sounds. Poor old Williams, our man, had the same wages as before, though he was well over seventy, but though his wages were small, purchasing power was happily high in those days. We raised our own pigs and poultry, which included ducks and turkeys—even a peacock went into the pot for chicken murder, he split their heads with a peck. We lived largely on poultry although butcher's meat was incredibly cheap and good. Our cook reported one day, 'Please mum, Willcocks can't eat turkey.' Willcocks was our garden boy and came from a very poor home.

My wife had a flair for animals, as have my eldest daughter and my granddaughter. The latter, many many years later, at the age of sixteen went to the New Forest alone, selected an unbroken pony for herself, broke it in herself to the saddle and was soon hunting on it.

My wife had resolved to keep a couple of cows, and before we left Southwell, had visited a model dairy with a great reputation, at York, where she learnt much. She had learned to milk as a child when she lived in the country. We had bespoken a beautiful little Jersey from a herd at Ilminster, Somerset, which was due for her first calf at the right date. My wife who had a gift for names, called her Amaryllis, the name of a country woman in Virgil's *Eclogues*, which had taken her fancy. The heifer was to be sent by train to Liskeard station, four miles from Duloe, and her advent was looked forward to greatly by us. My wife went to meet her new friend, and to lead her home from Liskeard station. The appearance of the rector's wife leading a cow through the length of Duloe village, caused an incredible sensation. The inhabitants peered at her through their windows; some stole to their garden gates to see this new thing. As the cow and her proud mistress passed out of sight, the inhabitants clustered together to discuss the portent. Judgement was passed, nem con—'No femmel, what called 'erself a lady, ud ever do sich a thing. Not un of our wenches ud do e!' The proprieties of Duloe were outraged. It was a frightful lapse.

Meanwhile, Amaryllis arrived home safely, had been inspected in triumph, and we, all unconscious, were enjoying in our tea our own cow's milk, for Diana had milked Amaryllis on arrival, and to milk the cow herself was what she intended to be her normal practice, and when she did not do it, I, if possible, took her place.

Diana had carefully digested what she had learnt at York, and then explained to old William the new order. He stared at her in amazement as she outlined to him our future practice and he made his comments in no measured terms. 'A suttificy from a vettynairy! Lor bless ye, what next? Heard tell of us for an 'orse, but a coo! Might have what? the consumption? Ha! Ha! Ha! but its so good as a play to hark 'e tell on un. I do feel fit to split, to think on't ...'

'Might be whisht (ill) without a cough! Lor bless 'e, s'long 's baist takes 'er mate t'aint no odds, cough or no cough.'

'What's it you'm after? ... Want d'drain kepp clear? Aren't no drain not what I knows on in t'linnhe. Anyways t'mooks cleared out every year. Never heard tell on the likes. Best let all bide together come May, when the

83

baisties lie out. I bain't goin' to meddle wid no sich things!'

'Wash an' broosh a coo! Eh, but 'e must be fairly mazed. But what was 'e reared to then? Us raids strange goings on in the newspapers, but this like do fairly bate un all.' Aside—'You'm bit soft mabbe!'...

'Milk and mate un regler? Drat un, ain't no odds an hour this ways or that way, an' s'long baiste gets 'er belly full 'taint in raison should make any odds...'

'What's that you'm saying of? Measure the mate of us? Eh, these noo fangled noshins!' (Aside) 'All mazed! the pack of ye, I'm thingin'.'

The extracts from an account of the reception of instructions by our old and inherited retainer are no doubt worked up, but on the whole fairly illustrate the impact on his mind. Poor William! We must have given him great shocks after fifty years with Canon Bush, a typical squarson. He felt coming to this very much. Diana as has been said had long since learnt to milk, and I had already learnt to milk a goat. That we could readily do these things was another shock.

I may claim that our farming was on the whole a success. We kept two cows, pigs, much poultry and bees. We lived largely upon the produce, and allowing for that (and we lived bountifully) the farming may be said to have paid for our man and our horse; it

84

involved a lot of work and made it difficult to go away from home—even when not anchored by the increasing family. It was not possible to leave my wife and the children without efficient help at night.

The dairy and the poultry run very much improved our fare. My wife made first rate butter, and Cornish cream was always on the table and the children could eat as much of it as they liked. The milk was also first rate and kept scrupulously clean. The surplus butter was sold at Liskeard.

In course of our time as our farming activities grew, I was invited to join the local Farmers' Club, which used to meet occasionally in Liskeard on Market Day, and I attended the meetings now and again. I believe that those meetings were not without value to me as a clergyman, and widened my acquaintance with my neighbours and helped me to understand the mind and point of view of the farmer better. At any rate it was, I think, approved. For the same reason I used to attend ploughing matches, and go to the tea afterwards. There was one at Duloe while I was there and the tea was followed by eighteen speeches, of which I contributed one, but it was the shortest. Celtic peoples have more natural eloquence than Saxons like myself and also more patience in listening. Heaven only knows what I found to speak on, as a speech from me was called for towards the end of the meeting.

The greatest event of my agricultural career was the winning of the third prize for mangolds at an Agricultural Show at Liskeard. It was grown on a large patch in our immense kitchen garden, which we ploughed, and which helped us to feed our cows and horse. It was amusing to hear the Liskeard tradesmen chaffing our farmers at being beaten by the parson at their own job. It was true enough that I grew the mangolds, but the selection of the exhibits was made by Philip Brown, who showed me which to pull and the grounds on which to choose them. I should never have realised else that shape counted for more than size or weight. The third prize which was allotted to me was not valuable—actually it was 3/6d, but it was real fun winning it.

The Church life at Duloe, when we went there, was reasonably vigorous. I have no doubt that Canon Bush had always a good standard of duty like many clergy of the squarson type and that had been quickened in his later years, so I was told, by a parish mission. When his strength declined, he obtained the assistance of an efficient curate, so the parish did not suffer, but I had to face a difficulty which had not existed for him. Some years earlier, in the days when the approved policy was to build mission rooms, one had been put up in a hamlet called Hill, between two and three miles from the rectory, on the other side of the deep valley of the West Looe. The service there was at 3 p.m. Hill could not be approached on a swiftly moving bicycle for a cause indicated by the name. I rode there each Sunday and hitched my steed up in a small stable by the church. The Hill service complicated Sunday School arrangements dreadfully, as now there were no grown up daughters or curate to help. For a possible congregation of ten I had to forego personal attendance at the Church Sunday School. The conditions as regards church going were very different from what they are now. I can remember one very wet Sunday evening when the congregation in Duloe Church numbered forty men and boys and three women. The church had then no competitors in a large country parish except the chapel. But these conditions have long passed away, with the advent of the car, the motor coach and motor bicycle and the competition of the cinema.

Dissent in our parish was fairly strong but not exceptional for a Cornish parish, and the dissenters, as they were called, soon united with us in many activities—the Nurse, Temperance, the parish room, churchyard improvement, and the like. When I began to improve the churchyard and advertised the intention by doing some work there myself, we invited the chapel to send a representative to the Churchyard Committee, as their dead lay there as well as ours, and dear old Mr. Hocken, their leader, was nominated by them to sit with us. That was, I think, very much approved. On Christmas Day and Good Friday it was always the custom to close the chapel and come to church.

Undoubtedly the religious division in Cornwall and probably largely elsewhere, was partly undesigned in early days. Evensong was almost universally in the afternoon and there was generally no evening service at the church. Certainly in many parishes the dissenters found their opportunity in an evening service, where the church had none. The clergy then moved their service to an hour, which they now realised was more popular than the afternoon and people had to choose between Church and Chapel.

The friendly tenor of Church life at Duloe was interrupted by one storm, which swept in suddenly when the sky was blue, and subsided as quickly as it arose. It all came out of a dispute utterly remote from Church life and after a few weeks there was a sudden calm. It became known as 'The Brown Fever'. At the moment it seemed to me likely to upset all our Church life, and being inexperienced I was almost in despair.

The farmers, who attended the local cattle market had been persuaded that the auctioneers were charging too high a percentage on sales, and that the charge must be reduced. This demand was likely to cause friction and it did. It so happened that a leading local auctioneer lived in Duloe parish and that the local secretary of the Farmers' Union was my churchwarden, Mr. Philip Brown—hence the name 'The Brown Fever.' There was no reason to suppose that the controversy would affect the church.

Our choir was in a very prosperous state. Actually it was overflowing, and when it was proposed that some girls should join there was no room to seat them in the chancel.

I was young and inexperienced and in my desire not to quench zeal, I suggested as a temporary arrangement that we might place a spare pew, which we had in store, in front of the front pew in the nave, and there these young women readily took their places. The occupants were thus seated in front of the seat where the Browns sat. Mr. Brown was churchwarden. Then whispering arose. It was rumoured that their behaviour was unworthy, and gossip connected the rumour with Mrs. Philip Brown. Very quickly the congregation, we might almost say the parish, was divided into hostile camps. On the one hand were the farmers, staunch to a man to Mr. Philip Brown; on the other hand the friends of the auctioneer; among them was our organist and choirmaster.

I scented danger at once, and sought to side track it. After consultation with the churchwardens, I told the girls that we proposed to remove the temporary pew and would ask them to occupy the rectory pew, which was level with the churchwarden's pew, and that Mrs. Bax would find a seat elsewhere. That seemed to be a fair offer, and of advantage to them, but no! Meanwhile the period of incubation had passed and the whole choir became infected with what was described as the Brown Fever. Underground influences were at work. It was reported that the wife of the churchwarden, full of naughty pride, had spoken unworthily of the choir. Meanwhile we had removed the pew.

On the next Sunday the girls sat at the back of the church, and I was informed that unless the seat was replaced, the choir would go on strike. On the Sunday after, the choir made a dumb attendance, sitting with the girls at the back of the church. But the church was packed and rang with voices raised in praise and canticle, and there was many a sidelong glance to see how the choir was taking it. On the next Sunday history repeated itself; the church was again packed, the singing would have done credit to a Welsh chapel. But it was time to make a move for peace.

As a first step I had a private talk with Peel, our squire, on whose friendliness and good sense I could always rely. We then talked with a young farmer, a member of the choir, and an interested churchman. They agreed that the time had come for a meeting. So we called a congregational meeting and asked the choir to attend.

On Monday the school was packed. I had developed a temperature of 102, but was of course in the chair. For the first hour there was Celtic eloquence but no progress. At last things reached a climax when a lady got up and said, 'Well! I've heard such things said by Mr. Brown of Mr. Olver that I could not repeat them. They were too bad to be repeated;' the silence that ensued for a few seconds was profound. Then Mr. Brown arose and requested her to say what it was. She murmured that she could not. 'It were too bad for repetition.' Mr. Brown insisted, and I from the chair, told her that she must do so.

There was dead silence, and she arose and while she cleared her throat there was a rustle through the room as people leant forward to catch every word she uttered. Then in a clear voice she proclaimed, 'I heard Mr. Brown say that he "had known better men than Mr. Olver".' For one more second the silence was profound, and then a roar of tempestuous laughter swept the room from end to end and died away and burst out again, as people rocked with amusement.

As people recovered, Mr. Olver arose, and with a twinkle in his eye and a smile on his face, said, 'Do you know, I think that I should be inclined to agree with Mr. Brown.' The day was won, but peace was not yet attained for the terms were not stated. We had yet to find a face saving formula. At last, sick in body and sick in spirit, I rose as the clock struck ten to postpone further consideration. Everyone was disappointed. The choir damsels were by now in tears.

I went home and was just getting into bed when there was a knocking at the front door. I put on my dressing gown and went downstairs. Bennet Toms and a member of the choir were there to tell me that an after meeting had been held on the village green and that a basis of agreement had been discovered. Would I return and put it to the meeting? They proposed that the seat should be replaced for four Sundays and the choir would then remove it themselves, and the girls would take their place in the rectory pew. The motion was passed with acclamation and was loyally carried out.

The final battle was fought at the Easter vestry. The room once more was packed, including some who never darkened the church doors.

Mr. Brown was proposed and seconded as people's warden. Then the auctioneer arose and pointed out that the notice of the meeting had been on the church door for one Sunday only and was therefore invalid. I asked if he wished to press the objection. He paused and looked carefully around the room, obviously estimating forces and then said that he would not press it. I then asked if the meeting was prepared to accept the notice as valid. Unanimously they answered 'Yes'. Then the schoolmaster nominated the auctioneer who was duly seconded. There were no other nominations, so it was a straight fight. The voting was very close—so close that there had to be a recount, but the result was the same—Brown by one vote.

That was the last of the trouble so far as the church was concerned, but before the Brown Fever died out the real issue was fought elsewhere, but that did not concern the church.

I have told the story at some length because it relates the only real parish quarrel that I have ever been involved in, and it had no rightful place in the church at all. In the end no harm whatever was done, and the Brown Fever became a matter of jest. Mr. Brown continued to be a parish warden for years after, to the great advantage of the church and parish.

I have only one other story to tell of the

choir. We had annually a choir and ringers trip and one year in our outing we passed through an old Cornish borough. We visited its noble church, and to their delight the ringers found the belfry open and the bells up. In a moment they manned them and their sound went forth to all the town, but not for long. A choirman arrived at a run. 'Stop those bells, and get away as fast as you can. The people are coming out of their houses in all directions like bees, asking where the fire is.' We had given a fire alarm! Happily we made our escape.

CHAPTER SIX

ACCOUCHEMENTS

We began life at Duloe with all sorts of good resolutions, but the days became more and more a hard but interesting drive.

The knowledge we soon acquired of the parish led to more work. Diana, before she came, had learnt much about village nursing from a friend, some years her senior, Miss Evelyn Eden, who had done a great deal for the cause of nursing in Somerset. Thus Diana's eyes were already trained to notice the need in Duloe parish, where the way would soon be open for a trained nurse. The

Goodie who officiated over confinements, was getting very old, and never, I think, resented the suggestion that, when she retired, her successor should be a registered trained nurse.

Diana asked the old Goodie if she would allow her to come with her to assist at a confinement, if the patient consented, that she might get to know at first hand what she was talking about.

Here is my wife's account of the first of these experiences, which reveal the realities of those pre scientific days with accuracy and sympathy. It is the picture of a confinement under the conditions then prevailing at Duloe.

It was May month. Every hedgerow, every steep bank and field had been until recently one pale sheet of primroses. Not that they were not there still in their thousands, but they were not so obvious. Long stemmed and paler, they leaned over the tops of the banks, peering into the deep rutty lanes. They were only the hangers on, the loiterers as it were, of a vast host, which had passed on. And even as they lingered the next great procession in nature's pageant had arrived. Drift upon drift of bluebells in the woods, alternating with drifts of snowy garlic, or ramsey as the country people call it. The blue and white were not mingled, but ran up the steep shoulders of the hills, the garlic white foam to the hyacinth's blue. And such a blue! Almost indigo in the cold bottoms of the valley, then purple blue, then sapphire blue, and when it reached the sun, azure blue.

The sun had long set however on the evening of which I write. The bluebells were invisible but their scent hung heavy on the grey misty air. Even the garlic was overpowered by the sweetness, and seemed content merely to stretch its white drifts round the curve of the valley. The well made winding road showed white in the dim light. It was bordered by steep banks fringed by succulent grass and backed by magnificent ferns. Down the steep road, somewhere about the hour of eleven in the evening, half trotted and bundled the quaintest of women. Her walk, if it might be so called, resembled nothing so much as the progress of a hedgehog. (My meaning will be clear to a naturalist. He will remember the back view of a hurrying hedgehog, and its consequential air.) She was evidently perturbed in mind, for she muttered aloud at intervals, 'Bless my dear heart alive, poor soul! poor soul!' These words were not said as smoothly as they are written, for Mother Bidgood's feet were tender and Mother Bidgood's elastic sided boots were tight, and the road was hard and steep. 'Poor soul, poor soul!' she exclaimed again and again, gathering up anew her bundle skirt of black stuff.

The road was evidently one she knew almost with her eyes shut, for, despite the black depths of the wood, she unerringly climbed the bank at the right place, and scrambled down a worn little track which led to a small cottage which was evidently her destination. She hurried round to the front, but before ever reaching it, she heard the familiar sounds, and exclamations proceeding from the little upper chamber. 'Oh Lord, I can't abear it. Oh whatever shall I do. Oh dear, ohhh!' A long drawn out moan ended in a sharp cry of agony. There was a noise of hobnail boots on the stone floor, and a man's voice said, 'Please to walk in.' Mother Bidgood did so, exclaiming, 'Hark ter that per soul up there. I'll be up in a minit, me dear.' She called in a kindly voice up the steep little stairs. Even the presence of another woman in the cottage seemed to bring relief, for the groans, though continued, were less despairing.

'Now, Mr. Rush,' said Mother Bidgood, taking charge at once as usual of the situation and the house, 'Yew please ter get some more sticks, and a nob o' coal, and get that there kettle boiling. I'll warrant yer wife'll take kindly to a drop of tea.' The man rose heavily and without a word, bent his shoulders and passed out of the door; and presently the sound of the chopping and snapping of sticks came floating in from the outhouse. Meanwhile Mother Bidgood quickly undid the strings of her bonnet, and removed it, and having carefully stuck the pins into it, she hung it on what was apparently the only available unoccupied spot, the knob of the little corner cupboard. Then she unfolded a clean white apron and put it on. After that taking up her little worn bag, she creaked up the steep stairs.

The little low ceilinged bedroom, crammed with useless odds and ends and with a mysterious heap of old clothes, was the very scene of discomfort. Those were the days before the advent of the district nurse or the registration even of old Gamps. Mother Bidgood's heart lacked nothing, but she had much to learn before she would have satisfied the standard of present day requirements.

Meanwhile Mrs. Rush, on seeing Mrs. Bidgood standing by the bed, turned her head wearily, and forced a smile across her poor cracked lips, showing a few discoloured stumps, which were all that remained to her, although she was but forty two. 'Eh but its glad I am to see your face,' she panted. 'The pains are awful. I was manglin' this forenoon when they came to I cruel. Oh!' She broke off with a cry, her face distorted with agony, and wildly clutched the fat hard arm of

Mother Bidgood, which had been stretched across her in an attempt to smooth the crumpled pillow.

'Don't mind me one bit, my dear,' said the kindly old thing, as with her disengaged hand, she extracted her not too clean handkerchief, and wiped away the great beads of perspiration that had gathered again on Mrs. Rush's forehead. 'There, there, don't e' cry,' for the poor creature utterly worn out with hard work and pain was feebly sobbing, her face turned sideways on the pillow.

It is often remarked by gently nurtured women 'that of course, cottage women don't feel as we do. I don't mean to be horrid, but just look at the families they have. Why I should simply die if I had to go through it again.' Would they? You will find that your cottage woman, the average cottage woman, is not given to complain or shirk pain. Mrs. Rush for instance was the mother of ten children. For fourteen years that woman had slaved, not simply worked, mind you, but slaved, night and day, in health and out of health. Imagine what it must have been not to have a single night unbroken rest for fourteen years. To have a baby, sometimes two, in the uncomfortable bed, and her husband as well, and never to get to bed till late every night, and to be up again at about five each morning. She was scarcely a woman to shirk these things, for she never complained, and if she did shed a tear or two when she found she was 'like that' again, she was the first to acknowledge when all was over, 'Why it's a big job to know how to feed him, but Lor! we couldn't do without 'em when they's here.' Yet this woman, who uncomplainingly worked on through the months preceding her lying in (and she suffered cruelly during those months) was the same woman who was writhing in agony on her uncomfortable bed. Sixteen shillings a week does not allow the purchase of any little comforts at such a time; and besides seven shillings and sixpence must be paid to Mother Bidgood after the affair. It was characteristic of a woman of her class too, that untidy and overcrowded as the poor little room was, still, at the bottom of the bed were folded two poor sheets, thin but scrupulously clean. Also Mrs. Rush wore a clean petticoat and a clean night dress, and greater reticence and modesty could not have been found in the biggest house in the district. Moreover, Mother Bidgood, with a knowledge born of practice for many a year past, went unerringly to the right drawer to find a little heap of coarse baby linen. It is true that the drawers were filled to overflowing with an indescribable collection of stuffy odds and ends and were difficult enough to open and still more difficult to close. But the poor little heap was there.

As the night wore on Mrs. Rush seemed to make but little progress, and Mother Bidgood with amazing frankness cheerfully opined that it was going to be a bad case; doubted but that she would have to send for the doctor before it was over; didn't rightly like the look of things; minded how in just such another case, the poor soul died before morning, 'Leaving just such another family as yours Mrs. Rush. T'was a cruel sad case.'

Mrs. Rush wept feebly at the recitation of these calamities, despite the fact that she had heard them many a time before, and presently expressed a wish that Mother Bidgood should step across to the other room and have a look at the other children to see if they were all right. It was as if the poor soul were fearful that the old woman's prophecies might come true. Mother Bidgood took the malodorous cheap oil lamp and went into the other bedroom. Here in its one large bed lay the children now at home—Bella, a not uncomely, strapping young woman of sixteen, home for a few weeks from service, lay on her back, snores and open mouth pointing to adenoids, from which two of the other children obviously suffered. The babies of the two previous years lay beside her in hot uncomfortable attitudes. The elder of the two was a rosy cheeked little fellow, but the younger was pale, with dark lines under the eyes. (It is the first eighteen months of a baby's life, commonly in the labouring classes, that is the most critical time. From that age or from two upwards it is little short of marvellous how the children pick up.) At the foot of the bed slept the other children, also restless and ill at ease, their turning and twisting betokening the irritation of vermin. Every now and again a hand would be quickly raised and the fingers literally tear among the rough untidy hair.

'Ah,' I hear someone say, 'however poor they might at least be clean.' Well I don't know. Have such things never occurred even among the pupils of select schools for young ladies, and have they not before now, penetrated into the sanctity of even the most guarded homes? And with what potions and lotions and washings and combings is not Miss Lucy's head treated. Sometimes even the family doctor is called in to assist, yet many a day passes before Miss Lucy is considered safe to mix with her little brothers and sisters or to come down to the drawing room. Now picture yourself the cottage home, when one day a child comes home with some 'insecks' in her head, another burden for the poor mother. If she be a slattern, she does nothing. If she be a self respecting woman as, thank God, the majority of cottage mothers are, what can she do but give Janie two pennies with injunctions to buy a tooth comb and a box of 'Mothers Friend' at the village shop on the way to school. But these are of little avail, for it is time that is wanting, and meantimes the affected Janie has distributed her 'insecks' to the rest of the family. Whereupon the resigned poor mother consoles herself with the well known adage, it is a 'sign of strength'.

Mother Bidgood was still lingering in the stifling little room with its damp stained walls and with the evil smelling lamp in her hands, when suddenly with a heart breaking cry, Mrs. Rush calls out, and Bella starts and moans at the sound. The old Gamp hurries across to the opposite room. There was no need for a doctor now she learned, for the familiar mewing cry of a new born baby greets her ear. 'Well, I never did,' she exclaimed. 'Bless my heart alive.' 'Be un maid or boy?' asks the weak voice from the pillow. 'Why he be a brave little lad, he be!' she answered. Then after burying herself for a few minutes with the baby and mother she takes her ancient scissors from a shabby hand bag and once more a little mortal starts his independent career in this hard world—wrapped around in an old flannel petticoat, and popped into bed feebly protesting. But poor Susie Rush is not yet through her trouble...

For Diana one lesson led to another. Mrs. Rush said that she wished that she had known more about babies before she had had her previous ten. All went merry as a marriage bell. The child grew and began to cut its teeth normally, instead of being toothless at fifteen months, as its predecessors had been. At eight months it presented the appearance of a healthy growing intelligent baby with straight limbs, firm flesh and a good colour. Then came a change. 'Please to come down at once, Baby's took terrible bad!' And the baby was terrible bad. It was repeatedly denied that any cause was known for the sudden illness. 'Perhaps the milk you sended down had summat wrong with it.'

But gradually it was wormed from the mother that 'Mrs. What was passing along and her looked in and said, "Big brave babby you've got, and teeth too. Hod'd rare un?" And then when I sez 'e has naught but milk and barley water she says, "Pack o' nonsense, not a bit of sense ter think a great babby like 'e can thrive wi'out summat to get uns teeth into!"'

And so the old sad story was repeated. A large cup of boiled bread was given to the poor little fellow, and within a few weeks, though the family tried hard to conceal the fact, the baby was 'sitting up to table 'aving mate and greens like any little man'.

Well in due course the registered nurse appeared and was accepted in Duloe and made her way and I think that the village mothers soon ceased to say—'for my part I dunno I'm sure what there is ter learn 'bout babbies'.

In the meantime my own family was increasing. Romola was born on July 13th, 1907 and Anthony on March 3rd, 1909. The night on which he arrived was bitterly cold. He came before he was expected and the nurse was not due for another week. About eleven o'clock in the evening as I was preparing to get into bed my wife told me that I must go at once for the doctor, who lived in Liskeard, five and a half miles away. I went out and saddled Briony. As we moved off she sat down. The ground was like iron and she was not roughed. It was clear that I should probably break my neck if I rode, so I put her back in the stable, and I pondered for a moment what to do. Our trained village nurse was happily by now a reality, and she was only two and a half miles away. I would fetch her first. I found her at home, and having put her in charge, I started for Liskeard. By now the snow was falling in a light powder, but by the time I reached Liskeard it had become a snow storm. I found the doctor and he promised to follow me as soon as he could. I returned in that whirling blackness of midnight snow which makes me feel as though in a dream. I arrived sometime in the small hours, long before the doctor who was also reduced to walking. All was well at home, and I was greeted with the welcome news that Anthony had arrived safely. I had walked sixteen miles that night mostly in snow after a hard day's work. A good cup of creamy tea made me feel as if I could start for Liskeard again, had it been necessary. It is well that it was so. On the next day, Sunday, I had to go to Lanreath in the evening, six miles each way to walk at the end of a long day.

My wife kept for four months a life history of Anthony. The record shows what a close observer of children she was, and it may interest other mothers to see some part of the record.

From a Four Months Record of the Life History of Basil Anthony Bax

Wednesday March 3rd, 1909. Basil Anthony born at 2.35 a.m. No caul. First baby who has been without one. Afterbirth not away until Dr. came, about 2 hours later. Weighed 9lbs 2ozs. Black hair inclined to curl. Not beautiful. Plump and well-made. Large hands and feet. Cried so long whilst we were waiting for Dr. Carter, that he was very drowsy when finally tidied up. Not very intelligent about sucking. Eyes somewhat swollen with crying. Did not open them much. Did not make as many aimless wavings with fingers as my other babies. Sucked thumb and wrist. Opened eyes more about 4 a.m. of same night. They seemed to turn towards the lamp, but this may have been imagination on my part. Cried somewhat latter part of the night, but nothing out of way.

March 4th. Anthony's eyes much less swollen. Seemed to be very drowsy, and disinclined even for food, tho' there was more for him towards evening. Snow and frost bad. Impossible to keep to regular two hours, as in deep slumber. Sucked thumb when roused a bit, but shows no intelligence about feeding himself. Had a good cry between 9 and 10, been drowsy during night. Spat out some nourishment which it had caused his mother the greatest pain to allow him to take.

March 5th. Anthony still more drowsy. Impossible to keep to 2 hours nursing, hence much pain for his mother. Eyes much less swollen. Moves his hands and feet far less than others. Charmingly shaped head, but face ugly. His ears lie flat as a dormouse's and he has a great space between his eyes.

March 6th. Anthony today moved his eyes much more, and stopped a grumbling cry when soothingly spoken to. As he did this twice it does not seem likely to be my imagination. He also frowned, and puckered his face when he heard a noise close to him. Seemed to be more intelligent in finding nourishment.

March 7th. 5th day. Anthony seemed to turn his eyes towards fire and candle as well as window. He fixed them on the face of nurse, just as if he could see her, and appears to gaze intently. He puckered the corner of his mouth into what she declared was a smile, and thought me hard-hearted for scoffing. Has a marvellous appetite, and shows no lack of intelligence now as to where to find food.

March 8th. Today Anthony seemed to take more interest in the light and candles and fire, and for the first time did not scream when actually in his bath, but appeared to appreciate the sense of warmth. He made up for it on being removed however. He seems to enjoy being carried a bit as long as he is held very firmly in arms.

March 9th. Anthony appears to have lost 6 ozs, but as I am not absolutely certain of weight of first blanket, I cannot be sure. Takes his food well, but spits out some. Most unlike our babies.

March 11th. Ninth day. Ant. seems to gaze

intently into one's face and to turn head decidedly towards direction of sounds made close to him. Places fist in mouth, with great accuracy and sucks furiously.

March 12th. Tenth day. A. had rather a bad night, and was rather snuffly. Today however he seemed to make a great step in intelligence. He deliberately turned towards any sound, and turned his eyes upwards when the sound was above him. He also stared fixedly at his mother whether he saw anything or not, and moved his eyes. Seems to have more control over latter than hitherto. He appreciated warmth of fire, and spread his toes like little fans to the flames. He gave two distinct crows of satisfaction.

March 13th. Had a very good night. Slept well during day. Crowed after bath by fire.

March 14th. Had fair night, 'snorts' better. Sleepy. Snowy outside. Has not stared about much, or made visible progress.

March 15th. A. seems very much older, and his face seems more ironed out. He distinctly turns towards anyone who makes a sound.

CHAPTER SEVEN

MORE OF DULOE

As I got to know Duloe, I realised how interesting the local history is and how far it carries us back into the past. In a field not far from the church is an ancient circle of eight stones, of which one has fallen and lies broken on the ground. It dates probably from the age of Stonehenge. Of the kind of people who erected and used it, perhaps the best picture is the description by the Roman General Paulinius of the forcing of the Menai Straits by his army in the year 61. 'The crossing was opposed by a strange and awe-inspiring assembly. Among the groups of warriors, women in ceremonial dress, bearing lighted torches, ran hither and thither and behind them were druids, standing by the fires of human sacrifice, their hands raised in prayer for help against the invaders. The Romans at first shrank from so weird a sight, then recollecting themselves, leapt ashore and fell upon the warriors, priests and women indiscriminately, and flung them into their own fires.' (Collingwood and Myres, *Roman Britain*. p. 98.) It was not a battle but a massacre.

Our stone circle at Duloe was very likely

erected centuries before that battle but I do not think that we shall be wrong in picturing the people and priest of our stone circle as akin to the Welsh army that opposed Paulinius Suetonius, the conqueror of Anglesey in the year 61. It is I believe accepted that an important feature of druid ritual was human sacrifice. Was the Circle at Duloe ever the scene of these horrors? It may well have been so. The Stone Circle at Duloe is out of sight from the church but what a lesson there is in the contrast and what a sermon! I wish that I had invited my congregation on some summer evening to adjourn to the Stone Circle and that I had there spoken of this great contrast—human sacrifice and Sacrifice of the Cross, the sacrifice of others and the Christian sacrifice of self.

The next phase of religion in Duloe has also left its memorial. As you approach the summit of the hill between Sandplace and the rectory, you pass on the left hand a spring known as St. Cuby's well. Here it is said that St. Cuby, the patron Saint of Duloe Church, lived and baptised, when he preached Christ in the neighbourhood. His success must, I think, have been quick and extensive. He is probably one of the two saints of Matthew Arnold's poem 'Seriol the Bright, Kybi the Dark, men said'. To Cuby or Kybi Duloe Church is dedicated.

111

Our next peep into the history of Duloe is the visit of Walter Stapledon, Bishop of Exeter, a man of fine character and great generosity, in 1324. He it was who worked for and gave generously to the building of Exeter Cathedral, and also became the virtual founder of Exeter College, Oxford. He came to Duloe to dedicate the church after its restoration, and two years later was murdered by the London mob.

There is much in Duloe church to interest the visitor and an account of it is given in one of those useful monographs, which we so often find in churches today, but I am concerned rather with the life of the parish in my day.

Most vividly there lives in my recollection, the Harvest Festival, then not simply a service of thanksgiving, but a cheery reunion of the parish to thank God and to renew kindly fellowship with each other.

It was so in my time and before, for we inherited this most real festival, a memorable day in our church calendar. The chief celebration was on a Thursday. In the afternoon there was a procession of children and a service at 4 p.m. The procession began out of doors. Then followed a parish tea, and the bells began to peal. Meanwhile a great fire had been kindled to boil the kettles, and its leaping flames lit up the Parish Green, around which were packed the vehicles, which had brought people from the distant farms. The service was held while the shades of night deepened, in a church crowded with people and beautiful with decoration. What a lot has been lost with the passing of a festival like that. It was a power for goodwill and fellowship and for the happy life of the parish, besides renewing the thought of God in minds in danger of being too much occupied in earthly things, and in profit and loss of a farmer's life.

In the church is recorded the list of rectors and vicars from Sir Nicolas Makerel (otherwise called Nicolas de Carleton) who is mentioned in Stapledon's Register (1318) as rector and Sir John Tregoit, priest, who was instituted to the vicarage in January 1336–7. The rectory was then a sinecure, and there was also a Vicar.

In the Great Rebellion Edward Cotone, the then Rector, son of a former Bishop of Exeter, went into exile. Of his successor, James Forbes, a Scotsman, Davies Gilbert, (Parochial History of Cornwall) sometime President of the Royal Society, tells the following story:

One Forbes or Forbhas was presented Rector in the latter end of Cromwell's usurpation, and lived here on this fat benefice, without spending or lending any money, always pretending want thereof; at length he died suddenly, intestate, about the

113

year 1684, having neither wife nor legitimate child, nor any relations of his blood in this kingdom; upon news of which Mr. Arundell, his patron opened his trunks and found about three thousand pounds in gold and silver, and carried it thence to his own house. The fame and envy of which fact flew suddenly abroad, so that Mr. Buller of Morval had notice thereof, who claimed a part or share in this treasure upon pretence of a noncupative will, wherein Forbes some days before his death had made him his executor, and the same was concerted into writing, whereupon he demanded the three thousand pounds of Mr. Arundell. But he, refusing to deliver the same, Mr. Buller filed a bill in Chancery against him—the said Mr. Arundell, praying relief in the premises and that the same money might be brought or deposited in the said Court, which at length was accordingly done; where after long discussing this matter between the lawyers and the clerks in that court, in fine, as I was informed, the court, the plaintiff and the defendant shared the money amongst them, without the least thanks to or remembrance of the deceased wretch, Forbes, for the same, abundantly certifying that saying in the Sacred Writing 'man layeth up riches but knows not who shall gather them'. This story is like a lantern turned upon a dark corner of English life towards the end of the seventeenth century, for Forbes died in 1684. Arundell and Buller represented two of the leading families of Cornwall and the third party of the transaction was the Court of Chancery.

The other story concerns the Rev. James Fincher, who became rector in succession to the Rev. James Forbes in 1684. 'Mr. Fincher had built a pretty fine house on the glebe lands of the Vicarage, equal if not superior to any other of that sort in Cornwall of its bigness, except Altar-Nun, as designing to buy the patronage thereof, being a sinecure, which I interpret too often to be, without care, thought, regard or guardianship over souls, where the rector presents to the vicarage. There was in those days both a rector and vicar of Duloe. But maugre all designs and endeavours of Mr. Fincher to purchase the patronage of this church, Sir John Seynt-Aubin and Mr. Arundell the patrons thereof, sold the same to Balliol College in Oxford in 1701. At the consideration of which fact, as common fame saith, Mr. Fincher was so dismayed, that forthwith he grew melancholy, and the grief thereof so depressed his spirits, that he broke his heart, and departed this life, 26th November 1703, at night, and so went to Heaven in that great tempest and hurricane that then happened, with many others.' It was on the same night on which Dr. Kidder,

Bishop of Bath & Wells, the successor of Ken the Non Juror, was killed by the fall of a chimney in the Palace at Wells, which to his High Church critics seemed to be a Divine judgement upon his intrusion into Ken's office. The unfortunate Mr. Fincher seems to have had an eye for landscape gardening, as well as for designing a home, for it was he who planted the beautiful avenue of limes. He was evidently a strong Whig for the choice of a lime tree was at that time regarded as a tribute to the House of Orange. That this avenue should lead only to the striking view of Tregarland Tor shows that he must have had a genuine taste for scenery even of that nature, which a little later might have been described as 'a horrid Alp'.

The most generally interesting of the rectors of Duloe was Robert Scott, afterwards Master of Balliol, who collaborated with Dean Liddell in the great Greek Lexicon—'Liddell & Scott'. He was instituted to the Vicarage in 1840 and to the Rectory in 1844, which thus became merged, and the endowment of £50 a year which belonged to the rectory, was transferred to the parish of Herodsfoot, which was taken out of Duloe. The study at Duloe is known as the Lexicon Room, and for a time Duloe was constantly visited by Dean Liddell, Benjamin Jowett and

Frederick Temple, afterwards Archbishop of Canterbury, who read for Orders with Scott. In the Marriage Register of Duloe there are entries of a wedding taken by Scott, and witnessed by two of these three distinguished visitors; the bride and bridegroom only putting crosses to their names.

Of Scott very little memory survived when I became rector, though between us there was only one incumbent, Paul Bush, who came to Duloe under medical sentence of death, and lived to be rector for fifty five years. The only memories that I could glean of Scott, as rector, were that he wore blue spectacles, used to go to Liskeard on Thursdays to choose his leg of mutton, and preached his last sermon from that unpromising text, 'I see a cloud no bigger than a man's hand'. The mutton and the blue spectacles are likely enough true memories (he had trouble with his eyes). One who knew him a few years later, describes him as a handsome man with a clear cut somewhat birdlike face, and of quiet kindly manners, under which lurked an irony which he seldom used. He accounted him as the most accomplished scholar who ever held the Mastership of Balliol, and of great tact and courtesy. Most probably these gifts counted for as much in a Cornish parish as at Oxford.

In a penny notebook Scott left some

jottings drawn up for the information of his successor, in which he reveals his character as rector. He was generous. He gave £400 for the building of Herodsfoot Church in a remote valley of the great parish and it is worthy of note that the list of subscribers included nearly all the Fellows of Balliol, Dr. Tair, afterwards Archbishop of Canterbury then head master of Rugby and A. H. Clough, the poet. He certainly had at heart, and was interested in, the welfare of the parish school, and described the head master as 'a painstaking but nervous man; his son John, as very clever but conceited and slippery, and the schoolmaster's wife as not overqualified for her place.' It does not appear that he taught in the school himself, but he says that 'the school was well thought of among the farmers etc., of which class they have several boarders.' 'The tenure of the school premises,' he adds, 'does not enable me to enforce such system and discipline as would be satisfactory, but there is no disposition to oust the rector from the general control of it.'

The church services, on Sundays, were at 11 a.m. and 3 p.m. or 4 p.m. according to the season. The Holy Communion was celebrated on the Great Festivals and on the last Sunday of every month. There was a service, apparently Morning Prayer, on Saints' Days and Ember Days and on

Wednesdays and Fridays in Lent. At first he had a lecture at 7 p.m. on Friday evenings, but he was obliged to discontinue it on account of his eyes failing him. He was also latterly unable to attend Sunday School as much as he would have wished as he found his Sunday work too much for him. He seems to have known his parishioners well and to have been careful of the sick. He says very little of dissent, but believes that John Grigg was the only farmer in the parish, who would think that there was any real difference in the point of right between going to church and meeting. In my day the chapel congregation came to church on Christmas Day and Good Friday. The change from an afternoon service to an evening service was apparently the wedge, which in many parishes must have finally cleft asunder the village religious community for then people had to make a choice between attending church or chapel. Frederick Temple in a letter to his mother bore testimony to the character of Robert Scott as tutor. On June 6th, 1840, he wrote, 'I do not believe there ever was a tutor who took so deep an interest in all entrusted to him,' and another penny notebook filled with his notes for the guidance of his successor, suggests the same care of his office as a clergyman. There may be found the accounts of Herodsfoot and the personal subscriptions to its building, the names of fifteen recipients of broth and two pensioners, the characters of farmers as tithe payers, indicating by cypher their quality as such; the names of the sick; the confession that he had carried away a china candlestick valued at 1.6d by mistake, and provision for payment for the same, a warning to have the dining room floor planed before laying the carpet, and a note that mice had nibbled the corner of every sheet of the Parish Tithe Award. It concluded with a careful inventory of wine in the cellar—'38 pint bottles of port, 11 quart bottles and 38 pint bottles of newer Do. 37 quart bottles of Sherry and 26 Do. of Marsala' concludes the information. It reveals a man who gave interest and care to all entrusted to him.

Of Dean Liddell I could discover little by parish recollection, but of Frederick Temple some memories survived. An old man told how one day when he was present at the school treat at which the future Archbishop was helping, Frederick Temple climbed a tree for the entertainment of the children, a practice to which he seems to have been given, but they were still more entertained when he tore his trousers so seriously that he had to retire to the rectory hastily to put on another pair. That was indeed a joke that children and parents alike would have appreciated. On another occasion he excited considerable surprise, if not mild censure, for his unconventional behaviour. There was a poor girl at the Rectory, who clearly was consumptive, for one night she had a bad haemorrhage. The future Archbishop ran to Looe for the doctor. That was no doubt approved of by the parish, but what they did not approve, was that he ran without his hat. The poor girl was buried at Talland. When opportunity occurred I found her grave still cared for in the churchyard there.

Beside our stock we had our pets and of those the more notable were Brown Willie and Brown Gillie. Here is their story, told by Diana:

'It is three years this March since they were hatched deep down in a red earthy Rabbit Burrow on the outskirts of a Cornish wood. Already the primroses and daffodils were showing streaks of pale yellow and darker gold where the green of the buds had parted, but for all that there were great patches of snow lying in the clearings of the wood, and along the shady sides of the red banks. Then they were brought to me "because you love babies and owls, and you've just got a new baby, and so we thought you'd like some baby owls." Clemency and Stephen explained it all to me so clearly. Quite true, I did love babies, and I had got a new one—just three weeks ago, and the last baby was only 19 months old, so now there were four babies to look after, and two cows to milk, and the butter to make, about 200 fowls and some turkeys to see to, to say nothing of the two pigs' daily rations to be superintended. Also plenty of village babies and mothers to help, and the thousand and one little odd jobs, that for some reason are supposed to fall naturally to the part of the parson's wife ... "So we were sure you'd like some baby owls ..." There was a hint of disappointment in the voice.

'Of course I was pleased. The children were quite right and after all if one is obliged to get up in the night to feed a human baby, one might as well feed two owl babies at the same time. So the two plain looking objects, covered in Jaeger-coloured yarn were ensconced in a small basket and tucked up on the last baby but one's shrunken vest. Every evening we put ready outside the window a little saucer of scraped meat—or minced mouse. Every night when the human baby was laid back in his cot, pink and milky and satisfied the owlet twins would stretch forth from the basket ungainly heads at the end of wavering and uncertain necks, and in due season they too would once more sink to rest with beaks reposing on alarmingly distended crops. And so the human baby, and the owl babies grew and throve, till the night came when it was clear that the owl babies were becoming so noisy and persistent before feeding times, that the human baby began to wake at all sorts of unauthorised times.

'"You are so fond of owls ..." "Yes, but when one has to wander downstairs to feed them at 3 a.m....!"

'However as time went on we found that a good feed the last thing at night lasted them till about six the following morning. In another three weeks we decided that they were old enough to "sit out". The human baby had "lain out" from the time when he was a few days old. The owl babies were therefore balanced on a curved branch of the old wisteria outside the dining room window. How many times one or other toppled off that branch during the first week I should be afraid to say. Every member of the household was pledged to see to them whenever their duties brought them to the front of the house. For their mistress they conceived the most demonstrative and violent affection. Naturally besides this, the apathy of her own new baby was most marked. Finally she used to crawl on hands and knees as she passed through the glass porch which was in full view of the wisteria. "I do declare I saw Mootie playing scouts s'morning all to herself," one small son joyfully confided to his brother. Indeed the greatest strategy was needed. If I did but pass the other end of the lawn, it caused such wild excitement that both owl babies would

123

violently hurl themselves from their wisteria perch. I would pick them up, and try to escape. Down they would fall again, and scramble and scuffle across the grass. Finally in despair I would feed them, and at least leave them blissful and lethargic. A few weeks later, but surprisingly late compared to other birds they began to change their fluff for feathers. Oddly enough the first feathers to push through were not on the head, back, and wings as with most other birds, but on their feet and legs. Day by day they developed first the most comfortable feather spats, and then neat and trim gaiters. The female grew by far the thickest gaiters, and of course, as is usual with birds of prey, was also the larger bird. Indeed she was a magnificent creature, and her feathers when they came were the richest chestnut, mottled, and barred with cream and white and dark brown. The last place to grow feathers was their heavy round eyelids which worked like the top of a roller-topped desk. It gave them an extraordinary appearance when they blinked, and showed numberless little feather paintbrushes, each in a tiny sheath. Being Cornish Brown Owls we had no alternative but to christen them Brown Willie and Brown Gillie. Their nest had been in sight of these two hills. They were shut up in a roomy cage under the old yew tree at night, but early in the morning the door was flung open, and with joyous squawks, their feathered legs hanging straight down, they would both gracefully sail out on to the lawn. Here they found a bowl of deep water and in and out of it they would go, splashing and shaking themselves until they only resembled the draggled ends of an old feather boa. When they were half dry they would fly heavily off to the lower branches of a Scotch fir. Another hour would see them trim and clean, every feather in place. Towards sunset they often used to sun themselves on the topmost boughs of the old lime avenue. They looked like two golden birds. If I came out of the front door they would straighten themselves, stoop, straighten themselves again, and suddenly float out into space the sun shining through their huge barred wings. They would never flap them once, in their descent to my hand. Sometimes it was dusk before I could call them in. On these occasions they were often most trying. One call on my part it is true would be answered by two tremulous hoots from some big tree, and when I was standing beneath the tree they would continue to talk to me but would seldom come down until I had tied my handkerchief in a knot, and thrown it on the grass. What attracted them in this performance I cannot imagine—for they never showed the slightest interest in the handkerchief once they were on the ground, but allowed me to pick them up. At other times it would be quite dark before I called them in. The darker the night, the further they wandered from the house. I would give their usual call, "Owlies! Owlies!" The answering hoots would sometimes sound far away. I never went down the lime avenue these evenings, but waited with my eyes covered, a very necessary precaution. Perfectly noiselessly the owlies would float from the far off tree and alight on my head or shoulders. Although one was expecting them every second, it was very startling when their sharp claws gripped one. Soon came the day when Brown Gillie made her first kill. A most exciting and interesting day for her mistress and no doubt for herself, but as the quarry happened to be one of her master's choice leghorn chicks, the rejoicings were hardly universal. I was so sure at first that she had found it dead, but soon had the gravest misgivings. Guilt, too, was written in those dark eyes as she looked back at me over her shoulder. Then still grasping the chicken in her terrible claws she hobbled away to the dark recesses under the yew tree.

'The following day "Brown Willie" brought me a mouse. He came sailing down the green dimness of the lime avenue—legs hanging straight down. I can see his bat-like flight now—wings seldom raised above the level of his back, but almost meeting beneath his body as he came noiselessly along. He flapped clumsily into my lap, for the mouse was scrunched up in his closed feet. He transferred it to his beak, and after crushing its skull, he dropped it into my lap, and began a game of trying to find it again. When he had done this a few times he dexterously turned it round and swallowed it whole— head first. After this he frequently brought me shrew-mice, but more for the fun of the thing than anything—as owls in common with cats will never eat a shrew. One evening I had a strange experience. I was slowly returning in the dark from a distant part of the orchard. Both owls were on my shoulder. Suddenly I felt Gillie's claws contract. She crouched, swooped, and in a second was up again flopping and tumbling against my neck. In her feet she held an unfortunate toad, her nails were deeply embedded in his back. I held her and ran with her to the house, Willie flying after us close to the ground. It was a curious sight. Gillie's gaitered legs hanging straight down, and the unfortunate toad "swimming" furiously in mid-air. She refused to let go, and finally flew off heaving into the bushes. She returned almost immediately without the toad. She can only have caught it for amusement, as no owl will eat one.

'Poor Brown Gillie! She was shortly afterwards harried to death by a party of young carrion crows, but Brown Willie is still as tame, and wise and affectionate as ever, although he later exchanged the green depths of his old Cornish home for the bleak and frosty north. Instead of the soft whirr of the nightjar and the call of the white and barn owl, across the wooded valleys, he heard on every side the clang of the shipyards, the rattle of the electric trains, and those unfeathered hooters, the huge voices that summon the men to the pits. Brown Willie's life did not finish in the north. He came with us to Maperton and then to Radstock.'

It was, I believe, through the teaching of John Wesley that teetotalism came to take high rank in Cornwall among the virtues, and with my Sunderland experience still fresh, I saw very clearly that the virtue of temperance was not as fully regarded as it should be in Duloe. Here too was an opportunity for church people and non conformists to work together, so we started a United Band of Hope with an adult branch. It quickly achieved remarkable success—so great that after a time the public house did not seek a renewal of its licence.

Temperance work alone would have been a poor policy for the public house is often the village social centre, so when the use of our public house was declining, it was necessary to put something in its place. After consultation we decided to build a village clubroom. Our squire gave us a site, and to save expense, on a suitable day at a popular hour, we met and removed the necessary length of hedge. Then we prepared the ground and dug the foundations ourselves. Peel, our squire, led the way and the young fellows worked with a will, including myself.

We collected in the new clubroom a sizeable library of really good books, which became very popular. That was in the days before the County Circulating Library was founded.

The mention of these books recalls the unhappy fate of a neighbour, a scholarly man of ecclesiastical tastes, and well read in the Fathers. To the regret of his parishioners, he announced that he had accepted a living elsewhere and was leaving shortly. They decided to give him a present as a token of remembrance. They knew that he was a reader and loved books, and the money came in well. The Committee determined to make the present as imposing as possible. When the day came their vicar received a complete collection of the works of Mrs. Henry Wood, some fifty volumes. I have often wondered what he did with them. If he put them in his study they would contrast queerly with St. Augustine or St. Cyprian. If he put them in his spare room his guest would judge him by them. The drawing room would be worse.

What if the Bishop or Archdeacon saw them. They might ruin his chance of promotion to an important living, for a well known proverb may truly take a slightly different form—'A man is known by his books'.

A ride which will always live in my memory was when the harvest was over and the work on the farms for a space was less pressing. It was a beautiful day in late summer when nature was preparing for her winter sleep. It was about three in the afternoon and I had strolled up to Tredinnick, our second village, to do a little visiting. Scarcely a soul was stirring, but the doctor's gig was standing outside the house of Charlie White, a master mason and a member of our eleven. Just as I came level with the house the doctor came out, looking worried. I stopped and asked if anything were wrong. 'Yes,' he said, 'the children here are suffering from poisoning and I must return at once to Looe for medicine, but I wonder if any others are poisoned. These children were at a party last night.'

'Have you got their names?' I asked. 'Yes,' he said, and then gave them.

'Very good, you go to Looe and get a bottle made up for each family' (happily only four or five in number). 'I'll get my horse and follow you at once and leave the medicine here and go on to Hill. You can easily deal with the others.' The farm at Hill was about six miles from Looe and quite isolated. There were two little girls there.

It did not take me long to get home and to saddle Briony and I was soon going down the steep hill to the station at a pace I had never before ventured. The doctor had got to Looe before me and the medicine was almost ready when I arrived. The journey was the same as I made every Sunday when I rode to Hill for a service, but we had never done it like this before, and I think Briony knew all about it and why we were in a hurry. There was no need to urge her. We had to slacken of course as we plunged down the precipitous hill into the valley of West Looe. A few Sundays before a viper had sat up on the hedge and hissed at me as I passed with my arm two feet from him. At the bottom of the hill it was a gallop again, but we slowed up for a space on the steep part of the ascent, and near the brow broke into a gallop once more. Very soon we reached the farm. Everything was quite quiet in the farmyard. Nothing stirred. Even the fowls seemed to sleep. I knocked at the door of the house. There was no reply. However, it was not locked, so I walked in and entered the kitchen. There I found the farmer and his wife. Each had a child in their arms. They were walking up and down the room, up and down, as though trying to soothe the children. They looked at me and said nothing, but continued to walk up and down, up and down, with eyes fixed on the child each carried. Their whole bearing spoke of their agony of anxiety.

I took the bottle from my pocket, 'Here,' I said, 'is what you want. Give the children each a dose at once. The directions are on the bottle.' It was an overwhelming reward to see the eyes that were turned upon me. I saw Hope driving out Despair. I did not wait, but slipped away.

The cause of the trouble was simple. A careless maid, in a well ordered farm with an excellent mistress, had mixed rat poison in a kitchen basin and left it imperfectly cleansed. Then she made a junket in it, which was set before the children at the party. Happily no one died, though one of the children in the farm I visited, was very ill.

The Cricket Club was a delightful feature in Duloe life. The squire of Trenant, Captain Peel, was a cricket enthusiast and the village club was in consequence in excellent condition. For neighbouring village fixtures we played our village team, but for the more formidable opponents we enlisted some Looe residents, as Looe had no cricket club. Dr. Webb, who included Duloe in his practice, was a really good bat. He had been in the Navy, but had seen from another ship, where he was lunching, his own ship, the flagship of the Mediterranean Fleet, H.M.S.

Victoria, rammed and sinking, and his shipmates drowning before his eyes. He was a very warm hearted man and could never go to sea again. Then there was Tommy Lang, once captain of Sherborne School XI, and a terrific hitter, who was tried for the County and would have been worth his place, but he had contracted a bad habit of hitting before he had taken measure of the bowling and leaving his crease in order to do so. It often paid in village cricket, but was sudden death when he tried it in a County Match. There was Crapp, the village carpenter, who bowled underhand—sometimes with effect, and their was Captain Peel himself, not a great bat, but one who would go in last, or nearly last, and often added some useful runs, and not a little excitement to the game by running unexpected byes. Duloe was a jolly team to play with and the field often rippled with jokes and laughter.

How I used to enjoy those matches!—the long drives through Cornish lanes, sometimes with Peel and sometimes behind Briony with one or two of the team with me, the game with its ups and downs, and the perpetual flow of fun. My cricket greatly improved—especially my bowling for I discovered a means of private practice. In front of our house was a circular piece of grass with the drive as the surround. On one side the front garden was bounded by a high bank above which was the kitchen garden. I pitched my stumps on the centre patch of grass with the wicket placed so that the ball would run up the bank and most of the way back to the bowler. I would then put a piece of paper where I wanted to pitch the ball and I quickly obtained far greater control of my length and command over the ball than I ever had before.

My greatest triumph was against a strong team of Looe visitors, captained by Doctor Webb, one of whom had recently won a Daily Mail bat and another played for a minor county. The day exactly suited me, but not the visitors, who were not accustomed to soft wickets. The match was played after a night of heavy rain and the pitch was sticky. They won the toss and went in first. I took the first over and Hawken, then the County change bowler took the other end as usual in our most important matches. My break from the off on the opening ball completely beat the first batsman, and my second ball was equally successful with his successor. Dr. Webb came in next. This time I overtossed a little and he sent the ball back very hard and low, but I held it and he flung his bat on the ground and swore audibly and continuously. I had opened the match with the hat trick, which I have not seen done before or since. Of course the wicket was all in my favour, but still I was very pleased with the performance. They made 26 and we beat them soundly. We were playing twelve a side. My batting also improved at this time, and at Maperton later on. Once, against Wincanton, I carried my bat through the innings and was not out at the end, but I never could see to hit, so my play was dull.

After a game at St. Germans, which we won after a good match, I was asked an awkward question. As usual I went in first. The scoring was slow on the pitches we usually played on, and it was so in this case. I was appealed against on the second ball for a catch behind the wicket and given 'Not out'. I made ten out of our winning score of about seventy. As we walked off the field, one of their team said to me, 'You were out, were you not in the first over?' 'That is not for me to judge,' I answered. 'Well! I thought you were,' he said. 'Did you?' I replied. 'We are bound to accept the decision of the umpire and it is hardly fair to him to reveal a mistake on his part.'

Well! I was out, but I would not tell him so, and I think I was right. If the ruling of the umpire is questioned even after the match, it would probably lead to questioning on the ground and quarrels in the next game, but it was bad luck on them. The umpire was not ours.

The village matches always afforded fun.

Peel had been in a regiment of Dragoon Guards. Although still young he had begun to carry weight. Undue modesty or his extreme regard for others made him go in last or nearly last but he became an expert at stealing byes. I do not remember that he was ever run out, but he galloped rather than ran up the pitch, but he ran with judgement. It was generally neck or nothing. His soldier servant, an ex Dragoon Guard, was also an exciting player. If he hit the ball it soared sky-high and as likely as not be a possible chance of a catch for someone, but it would be descending from the sky and was often not held.

CHAPTER EIGHT

LAST DAYS AT DULOE

As I became known in the Liskeard district, various small offices came to me. I was invited to become one of the assessors in the adjudication of income tax appeals in the neighbourhood. It was my practice not to refuse work like this, even though remote from my office. Such occasions bring experience and contacts, which have their use and value.

What was more important was my

selection to be a member of the Liskeard District Education Committee. In those days the Cornish County Education Committee worked through six district committees, of which Liskeard was the centre of one. Our Chairman was no less a person than 'Q', who had not yet become Sir Arthur Quiller Couch. We had already come into contact in the Diocesan Conference, where we found ourselves in general agreement. On October 27th, 1908, he wrote of a meeting, 'I wish you luck. Writing novels is far better fun anyhow than talking to a Diocesan Conference. They were beautifully kind; but I own that the speeches left my hopes depressed, especially the oration of Canon X, who is by the way quite a good fellow. It sickens me to see the Church fighting points like a borough corporation, when with proper courage she could open her arms and smother, positively smother her enemies in one great jolly maternal embrace. Very likely this strikes you as rot, but I should very much like to defend it over a pipe.' The allusion to writing novels was to an effort of my own which I had attempted in the vain hope of making a few pounds that I badly needed. It was not successful but came very near to being productive. One of Q's comments on it is amusing—'There is apt to be a prevalence of gloom in first novels. I should be sorry to count up the number of quite worthy people I massacred in "Dead Man's Rock".'

I fear it was supremely so in mine. I placed the concluding disaster in Mount's Bay and the last scene is in the vestry of a Church, which may have been Breage, 'Then they went into the vestry and he (the Vicar) took out the burial register and found the entries for 1793. As he ran his finger down the page he stopped at the date September 7th and read, "Six of the crew of the *Ganges*, Indiaman, which struck on the Staines and foundered with all hands on Friday evening, September 5th, during one of the most furious summer storms ever remembered. All of the crew perished."

'On September 8th there was this further entry, "Two seamen, names unknown, supposed to be part of the crew of the *Ganges*, Indiaman. Also two more parts of bodies at the same time." Rachel turned away with a sickened feeling as she read the words.

'"Here is one more entry relating to the Indiaman," said the rector, "and I think it may throw light on the subject of your inquiry. See here under September 9th," he added, turning over the page, "a man and a baby girl, names unknown. The body of the man was washed ashore with the child clasped in his arms."'

'Later in the day the rector took her down

138

to the cliffs. The ship, he said, was embayed here on that September night in a westerly gale. "There was no hope for it except from a change of wind. The *Ganges* struck there on the Staines. Do you see where the waves break into foam about a mile from the shore? It is so calm that the spot is well marked today. By those rocks the Indiaman lies and it was there upon the sands of Pra that the tide brought to the shore the bodies of Mr. Richard Jephson and little Molly."'

The book was gloomy but it was not untrue or exaggerated. An Indian civilian told me that he picked up the book to see how many mistakes I had made about Indian life and that he could not find one. I had been very careful to study journals and letters of the period concerned.

The last letter I received from Sir Arthur Quiller Couch is dated July 15th, 1910 and was in reply to one in which I congratulated him on his knighthood, and suggested half mischievously that he had better stand for Parliament. He replied, 'It was very jolly of you to write and you'd forgive my untidiness if you could only see the pile of letters which took me literally even more of a heap than the small honour itself—though that dismayed me enough. You will never congratulate me anyhow upon entering the House of Commons, nor even at being defeated at a poll, though that were a better excuse. For indeed I should loathe the whole business, and—though you may smile—it is true that I detest even local politics. Got mixed up in them simply to start with because the war in South Africa made me angry and the concentration camps made me wild. But when a man gets a foot into the quag, it's odds that one's whole leg follows at least. I hope you are happy up in the north, and won't mind my telling you it's a fact that I have never seen Cornwall more beautiful than it is this summer. Our small garden has beaten all records and horrible millionaires stop their motors to see in and enquire the name of one particular rose. I delight in telling them that it's a common musk and cost me 9d and should like to add that they can easier go through the eye of a needle than grow the like.' The beauty of Cornwall remembered in less kindly surroundings has often made me a stranger wistful. He was a Cornishman and how deeply he loved the county.

About this time before we left Duloe the following incident is recorded in an undated letter written by my wife. My eldest daughter remembers it well. 'Poor Clemency is very sad. She woke screaming in the night saying, "My darling little canary is dead". It took me five minutes to stop her sobs. This morning as if to comfort her it sang for the first time for some weeks, but it has been perfectly well. She noticed that it had a little piece of cotton on its leg, which it did not resent having removed. Afterwards, with seed still in its mouth, it fluttered across the cage and fell dead in Clemency's hand without a struggle. Isn't it extraordinary. We are all so sad. I had him long before I married. He was apparently perfectly well.'

We were never long at Duloe without some adventure. One night when I was absent at a social entertainment in the village, the servants reported at eleven p.m. when they returned that a man was lurking in the back premises. Diana called Hecate, a French poodle, and immediately went out to seek him. They found him near the stable and challenged him. He tried to make off, but with the dog's help, she cornered him in the stable yard and extracted his name from him. He proved to be a quarryman in a somewhat fuddled condition on his way home from Liskeard and was carrying two charges of dynamite in his pocket.

One of our most serious adventures in Duloe, perhaps our greatest—more dangerous than the unsupported arch of the bow window in the drawing room—was a prolonged threat of fire. One day Clemency was sent up to the attics to fetch something, and returned with the disturbing news that they were full of smoke. We went upstairs and searched for the cause, which we traced to the dining room chimney. I spent part of that night on the roof which I was able to reach from an attic window, where the back premises adjoined the main building at a right angle. From that point the chimney was easy to reach and bucket after bucket of water was handed to me from the window out of which I had climbed. None of the water reached the dining room, but returned upwards in clouds of steam. We had the chimney swept and it was pronounced safe.

On April 8th, 1908, I wrote to my mother—'I was away preaching last night and arrived home this morning to find the chimney on fire. After breaking four holes through a wall, we found that an oak beam which formed part of the chimney was in flames. It must have been alight and smouldering for a long time. However all is safe now.

'The boys have each bought a pig as a speculation and I found them both incarcerated in the pigsty this morning. They had gone in "to view" their pigs and the condition of their home, and Clemency shot the bolt while they were looking at their new ventures.'

The next recorded event is dated December 26th, 1908, when I wrote, 'We commemorated Christmas in an unusual way. Without rhyme or reason last night our bedroom chimney burst into flames. Luckily we got it out and it was not a beam this time, thank goodness. The chimney was swept at the beginning of last month.'

The final occasion was Easter 1909. My wife wrote—'We have not seen much of Arthur of course, as his work on these kind of days begins by riding out to Hill between 6 and 7 a.m. and he is not home for good until after the evening service. He's awfully tired by that time, and yesterday he had then to make explorations among the chimney pots.'

The final fight with fire must have come soon after. The story is recorded in a letter from which the date has been torn off. The chimney was alight again. This time it must be a fight to a finish. We sent for the mason and carpenter. The former removed the wall above the fireplace until we could reach the beam, from a bedroom on the first floor above the dining room, which was glowing dully. As soon as the mason had accomplished his work, the carpenter with an axe chopped away the burning wood from the red end of the oak beam. As each piece fell, I threw it into a bath of water. This process was continued until there was room to cut the beam off entirely from exposure to the sparks in the chimney, by walling it in. Thus the battle was won.

The old beams were actually built into the chimney itself and must have been charring for years. They say the place was red hot all round, and must have burst into flames by night. The draught made it do so at once. While there was only wood fires, the sparks went up the chimney. It was the change to the use of coal with its soot that was the cause of the danger.

A feature of my years in Cornwall was the ruridecanal chapters which met periodically under our Rural Dean, Canon Aldham, Rector of Boconnoc, and very pleasant was the ride to the homes of our different hosts in that beautiful district—the deanery of West. We would gather for lunch and stay for tea and the food was indeed a contrast to that of today. The clergy were a very nice set, some of them of the squarson type, and all would listen patiently to views with which they disagreed. We had a sharp engagement over 'the Deceased Wife's Sister Bill', and nearly carried a resolution in its favour which was almost unheard of then. They treated me with kindly tolerance when I showed signs of trying to set the world right with youthful zeal. I remember raising the question of absenteeism of which there was an example in the deanery, and on another occasion I voiced disapproval of the purchase of a living, though it was very disagreeable to do so. I felt strongly that these abuses would never cease unless people spoke up. The clergyman in question behaved with great

144

grace. He had spent many years as a chaplain abroad and family circumstances had necessitated a return home. No one offered him an opportunity, so his wife purchased a living. He was a very nice fellow and a good parish priest and we became very good friends. I did not like to do these things, but I felt strongly that unless public opinion was created, there would never be reform. I chose my words carefully, and the older clergy seemed to listen with amused tolerance.

I was invited to join a society which held annually a two days meeting at Truro. It aimed at freedom from all party spirit in its meetings, but as it was bound by a rule of silence for both days, there was little room for a display of self restraint. I proposed that we should be allowed to talk on one of the two days. I explained that I came from an isolated parish and this meeting was an opportunity for me to achieve improvement through the conversation of my friends, but how could that be if we were not allowed to talk to each other. I carried my resolution, but at the next meeting the old order was restored, for some of the members had become very plaintive, almost lachrymose about the change—'it would spoil the society for them' they affirmed.

During my years at Duloe I taught my children for a time myself. It was no easy task. Stephen learned to read fairly easily. Clemency, his twin, had inherited her mother's practical and not a little of her artistic power, but she would not learn to read and it was long before she could do so with ease. Oliver learnt without being taught.

As I saw that the relations between England and Germany were becoming central in world politics, we procured for them a German girl from Brunswick as nurse. She learnt English but they no German. Then we got, as mother's help, a girl from Darmstadt, whose father was manager of a big bank there. She was first rate and became a great friend. Stephen learnt some German, enough to help him to learn Dutch easily in South Africa, Clemency some, and Oliver to speak with reasonable ease.

With Stephen I drove down to Breage on Mount's Bay—54 miles, on a Monday and home again on the Thursday. Briony did the journey of 54 miles well. It was very hot as we passed through Truro and we drew into a wayside wood and I took all her harness off and let her have a good roll and graze while we had tea. After that, as the day cooled, she went beautifully. At Breage we stayed with the Rev. H. S. Coulthard, a great friend of mine, who had written an excellent Parish History—'Breage with Germoe'. In the church, where wall paintings were already exposed, they found later a huge figure of Christ as Piers Ploughman. From the five wounds the blood of Christ flowed over the implements of daily toil, thus signifying the consecration of labour. The subject is said to be an almost literal illustration of certain passages from Langland's great poem. It represents a people's Christ and reveals the existence even then of that amalgam of religion and political revolt, which seems to have been always present in Cornwall.

On the way home on Thursday Briony would hardly stop to eat. When we arrived she started grazing while I was washing down her legs in the field.

Later on Stephen and I had another driving expedition together in North Cornwall. They were the beginning of many expeditions with the children at home and abroad. They were designed and, I think, did play a real part in their education. They were meant not only to open out their minds, but to teach them how to look after themselves, and to approach in a friendly way strangers of any nationality.

For some time we had been troubled about Oliver. At Southwell he, as an infant, had shown signs of asthma. At Duloe this was now becoming more pronounced and we were getting very unhappy about it. The warm Cornish climate and our many trees did not seem to suit him and I told my trouble to Balliol, and one day a letter arrived offering me the living of Long Benton, which is in the near neighbourhood of Newcastle upon Tyne. I had become very attached to Duloe and my wife, who in particular was much criticised at first for her part in our farming efforts, had outgrown that phase in our Cornish life. When the district nurse arrived people had begun to realise what a true friend they had in her. It was sad to leave Duloe but we felt that we must venture for Oliver's sake. So I wrote and accepted the living of Long Benton. It was a great venture.

I was greatly touched when I told Mr. Hocken that I was leaving. He was the leader of the non conformists, and was their representative on our churchyard committee. To my dismay he burst into tears, saying, 'With you here, we have had five years of peace.' It is my conviction that when reunion comes, it will come through friendliness and co-operation and not through argument; not by conversion of one party or the other, but by a deepening sense that we are all falling short of the Spirit of Christ, and his spirit is the spirit of Unity.

Our last morning had come and we were ready to start for Devonport, the first stage of our journey north. Everything was ready and there was a full half hour to spare. I strolled into the garden in a purposeless way, and looked at my watch again. Yes! there was plenty of time. I would visit the dear old church once more.

As I turned off the high road to Liskeard, I saw Bill Tamblin beginning work on a new heap of stones, which had been tipped by the side of the lane to Hill, which skirts the green outside the church. He was standing leaning on his hammer with his old wideawake pulled down to shade his red face. I at once turned towards him and extended my hand. He took it in his and stood for a few moments holding it in silence, like a man trying to say something which he finds difficult to put into words. Then words came—utterly unexpected words!

'I should like to take the Sacrament with you before you leave.' My heart leapt as I heard them. Never had he entered the church while I had been there.

'There is nothing I should like better,' I said, 'Come into the church and I will place you in your seat, where you must wait for a few minutes, while I fetch the vessels and the bread and wine.' I seated him in a chair, which I had placed in front of the altar.

So this summed up our five years of friendship and the amusement we had had together—he trying to teach me to crack stones, and I labouring to get him on to the governess cart. There in that ancient church with hundreds of years of history behind it, we partook together of what was one of the most unexpected communions ever celebrated there—and one of the most real.

Together we partook of the bread and wine and that was the last time we met on earth, for shortly afterwards he died.

Who can fathom the movement of God's Spirit in the hearts of man! 'The wind bloweth where it listeth, and thou hearest the sound thereof, but canst not tell whence it cometh nor whither it goeth.'

Why did I return to the church? I do not believe that it was through what people call chance. I believe that Bill Tamblin, when he came to work that morning felt an urgent desire to take the Communion with me, and this desire reached me in the form of a call to revisit the church. Spirit conveyed its message to spirit. The communication passed, though it was never uttered by the voice of man.

I do not think that my return to the church was a matter of chance, but a case of telepathy, mind communicating with mind at a distance.

As a boy of eighteen I became a convinced believer in this power. I was staying with my mother in a cottage we rented on Dartmoor near Princetown and my sister was at home in our house in Devonport. One day about six o'clock in the morning my mother came into my room and woke me up. 'I want you

150

to get up,' she said, 'I know something is wrong at home, and that Maggie (my sister) wants me very badly. I must catch the 8 a.m. train and I want you to take my things to the station.'

When she arrived at our house in Devonport, the door was opened by my sister, who cried out, 'Oh mother, I am so glad to see you. I have been wanting you so badly. The cook has gone mad and I have been sitting up with her all night.'

CHAPTER NINE

LONG BENTON

We left Duloe on a sunny November morning and stayed for two nights with my mother in Devonport. By the time we reached York a light powdery snow was falling. At Newcastle there was a snowstorm. However, our party of five children and ourselves, a German governess and two maids, a goat, two cats and an owl, reached Long Benton without serious misadventure, but for the next few weeks, the children seemed to spend the day eating bread and butter, so affected were they by the change from Cornwall to the bracing air of the North.

151

Our new parish lay between Newcastle and the coast, and to the north of the Tyne. Across the flat country the northeaster raged unbridled in winter and spring. In summer a few hours of glorious sunshine was generally followed by a grey shroud of mist from the North Sea. The climate was certainly bracing. I know of no place in England where a man, tired in mind and body, can be restored to vigour more quickly than on the pier at Tynemouth, by a few brisk turns from end to end. The shortness of the winter day is not compensated by the prolonged daylight of summer.

Our vicarage, in the old village of Long Benton on the road to Newcastle, was old and roomy, and unlike Duloe rectory had little history but the connection of the parish with Balliol College carries one back to 1260. In that year an outrage was committed by John Balliol the father of the claimant to the Scottish throne, on the Prince Bishop of Durham, which was expiated by receiving public chastisement at the hands of the Prince Bishop of Durham, in front of Durham Cathedral and being condemned to giving lands for the foundation of a college at Oxford. John Balliol died—whether the shame of the chastisement or its severity contributed to it, we do not know, but very shortly after her husband's death his wife Devorguilla handed over, in accordance with his sentence, three farms for the foundation of a college at Oxford. Balliol College was thus founded and those lands are still in the possession of the college. In my day they were still farmland, and so far as I know they retain traces of their primitive character.

The parish church is in the geographical centre of the ancient parish. In former days it stretched to the Tyne, embracing what is now Wallsend on the one side, and on the other the parish of Killingworth. Across the Glebe of the then vicarage of Long Benton, George Stevenson, the Killingworth engineer, tried out the engine, which pioneered perhaps the greatest change in the aspect of England that our country has ever known.

In days not long past the church stood alone, save for a room where farmers spent together the hours between morning and afternoon church, and a stable in which they could tie up their horses. To this a house was added later, for a verger to enable him to keep watch on the churchyard in the days when body snatching was rife.

When the electric railway line was constructed from Newcastle to the coast, a station was being built near the church and houses were being fast built there and also at Forest Hall, through which the main line to Scotland passes. It was of great interest to my family, fresh from the wilds of Cornwall, to walk to Forest Hall and to stand at the barrier gates and see a great Scotch Express roar across the level crossing, a few feet away. They seemed to a child standing on the road peering through the gates, enormous in size and terrifying in power and speed.

Between Long Benton and Walker and the Tyne was a worked out colliery, known as Biggesmain. Around it lived some old people in cottages, some of whom, perhaps all, in years gone by had worked at the colliery. We had there a small mission room, where we held a weekday service.

Biggesmain, as it was called was now derelict. It was not only the ruined buildings of the mine which testified to that. The land around seemed to have lost fertility. It was not tilled, and no cattle grazed there, but the mine no doubt had made somebody's fortune, and kept others warm, but when I saw it the land was useless. Hard by the ruined engine house was the pool, from which its water had been drawn, unfenced and sinister. While I was at Benton two small children had been drowned in it.

Biggesmain in the middle of a prosperous neighbourhood was a sinister reminder of the danger which threatens a district that depends only on a colliery.

One day as I was walking along the path which led to the mission room and cottages

154

on a bitter evening when it was blowing hard from the north east, I saw in the leafless thorn hedge a poor white parrot which had escaped from its home. I tried to persuade it to step on my hand but it flew away. I hope that it flew homewards, but I could not stay to do more for I was pressed for time.

Sunshine and shadow played across our path. Happily, I could not foresee that which was to come. The congregation was very friendly and the work was interesting. I inherited a most successful church council founded at a time when they were a novelty. In some ways the meetings were a model. The members were all businessmen and, like most north country men, knew the value of time. As the hour (8 p.m.) approached on the night of the meeting, the secretary would stand, watch in hand, and immediately it struck eight, he used some formula like 'Go', and go we did, whether the chairman was there or not. They were prepared to find time for church work, but they would not have their time wasted. This practice suited us very well. The vicar's warden, who was chairman, was Professor Thornton of Armstrong College—a tower of strength to us and a great personal friend.

At my start in Long Benton I became involved in a serious business worry. A large part of the income of the benefice was derived from the colliery wayleave across the

Glebe, the rent being a certain sum a year, and 25 tons of coal. In accordance with ecclesiastical law the lease expired with the resignation of the incumbent, and had to be renewed when the vicar was instituted. Meanwhile the colliery company naturally went on using the wayleave. We on our part wanted some coal to go on with. Why buy? when presumably the lease must be renewed and in any case it was being used at the moment. I went to the colliery office, looking for no difficulty. Would they, 'without prejudice to future arrangements,' send us some coal for use pending renewal of the lease? Unhappily the manager was out and my reception was not friendly.

I went to the college agent and he took me to the college solicitor and shortly I found myself involved in the internecine strife of two colliery companies. There followed an action before Mr. Justice Grantham. The affair did not take long. 'The vicar,' he explained, 'had come from the south and here of course he was cold. Why should he be refused some coal without prejudice to future arrangements, when, in the meantime, the wagon way was actually being used' etc. We won the action, but what I wanted was a settlement and peace. The way to this was not opened until a dramatic evening meeting was held which I brought to an end by announcing that unless peace were made, I should resign and thus automatically open the way to a settlement. After that all was well and I found myself on the best of terms with both parties, but the anxiety it had caused me was trying and the whole dispute had been utterly needless.

Comedy meanwhile became mingled with graver matters. My eldest son had joined his cousins, George and Michael Lawrence, at a school at Eastbourne. They, as before, came to us for their holidays while their parents were in India. We met them at the central station and found three dejected small boys, not at all like boys returning for Easter. Whatever is the matter? we asked, and then they told their story. They had armed themselves with a pea shooter before they left London, and as the train slowed down while passing through Peterborough, Michael took aim, fired a shot and hit an old gentleman on the chin, who was standing by the bookstall. The missile was a pea. At any rate it stung him up, and naturally furiously enraged, he danced off to the stationmaster. As the train drew up at Grantham, the boys were much interested to observe a posse of police and railway servants on the platform who boarded the train. The boys' interest became consternation when the posse thronged into the compartment where they were seated, and told them that they had killed the old gentleman, and asked for their names and addresses and pistols, assuring them as they received them, that the matter was not going to rest there. They left the boys very despondent. The cheery holiday mood had gone beyond recovery—for a time. No wonder they were piano when they reached Newcastle, but, as the days passed, they recovered their usual spirits.

A few days before the holidays came to an end, I took the boys and my eldest daughter to the Lakes for two or three days' scramble on the mountains. As we got into our carriage at Benton, the Irish stationmaster, who was a friend of theirs, came up and mysteriously pointing over his shoulder with his thumb, said, 'There's a detective from York asking for your young gentlemen, what shall I say?' 'Tell him,' I replied, 'that they've gone away.' The train moved out of the station, leaving the detective from York in conversation with the stationmaster.

We returned in a few days to Benton, and, a day or two after, they went back to school. The day after they had left, as I was working in my study, I heard a ring at the door, and I at once felt certain that it was the detective from York and the maid ushered in an impressive looking man in a frock coat, who introduced himself, as I expected, as the detective from York, and at the same time he handed me his card. I looked at it. The name was familiar. My mind travelled back to

Sunderland. I remembered there a neighbouring vicar of the same name, a corpulent but sturdy old gentleman, whose hobby was to take degrees at different universities. I think he hailed from Cambridge originally. One day he caught a burglar in his house. The man struggled in vain in his strong grasp, and as help was approaching shouted, 'If you don't let me go, I'll butt your guts out,' but the old gentleman had him firmly and handed him over to the police—a very good performance for a middle aged man who was rather stout.

'I have come about the shooting affair,' my visitor explained. I asked him to sit down and enquired if that vicar whom I had known in Sunderland was a relation of his. It was as I surmised; he was my visitor's father. I had some faint recollection of hearing that a son of his had joined the police force at York, with a view to becoming a detective. Our conversation passed from my family to his, and to Sunderland. At length I enquired, 'Are you married?' 'Yes.' 'Have you any children?' 'Yes.' 'Any boys?' 'Yes.' 'Then I expect you know all about boys?' He laughed, and said, 'Yes. I do.' Then I said, 'Well, what about this shooting affair?' 'Well,' he replied. 'If you will allow me to keep the pea shooters and you undertake that the boys will not do it again, I think I can promise you that they will hear no more about it.' 'I think I can safely do that after the fright you have given them,' I replied. He laughed and at that we parted.

The Bishop came to visit us in the late summer to take a Confirmation. We were having a meal and the window, through which on clear days we could see the Cheviots, was open. The churchwardens were of our number. Suddenly a pair of starlings flew in, circled the room and alit on the Bishop's head. They had been taken from the nest and brought up by my wife. He took it very calmly, and exclaimed— 'Gracious! What next?' 'A pair of jackdaws, I expect,' said my wife.

Another amusing incident was a conversation with a neighbour who had a weakness for whisky. Like many another he was a decent enough fellow on all ordinary occasions. Once at least I emptied all his whisky that I could lay hands on out of the window, as the shortest way to put an end to a difficult situation. He bore a very unusual name. One day I met him plunged in deep dejection. 'What's the matter?' I asked him. 'My dear Bax,' he replied, 'it's a damned business having a name like yours or mine. If we get into a bit of trouble with the police, everybody knows at once who it is.' He was so upset that I did not venture to suggest that he might change his name to Jones or Smith at small cost by deed poll.

One parishioner presented an interesting study. He was ninety years of age, and I suppose that the world would describe him as a successful man. He had started life with next to nothing, but he achieved a very great fortune according to all accounts. He had made a mass of money by what he called 'specilation'. Its foundation was an investment at an early stage in a great north country ironworks. When I paid him a visit whatever subject I tried to open up, we were again in a few minutes talking of the ironworks. We always came back to it. He had quarrelled with his family and friends, but a nice little granddaughter looked after him. He lived in a street of small artisan houses. Normally he gave nothing away, but to my knowledge he once made a handsome gift to a hospital. He had attained great financial success, but his soul seemed atrophied and his life empty, except for his one interest. I wonder what became of his money. I hope that it passed substantially to the family, with a good legacy to that nice little granddaughter.

Professor Thornton had a family of about the same age as ours and we made some very pleasant expeditions together and in one we played hide and seek in the old castle of Warkworth. I had noticed that the great chimney of the main room was perfectly clean, so I ascended a short way up it. After a

161

futile search for me they assembled close to it to discuss what could have happened to me and what steps they should take next. I relieved their anxieties by crowing from the chimney. Many years later I was informed that Warkworth Castle had been a stronghold of my wife's ancestors—the principal residence and possession of the House of Clavering c.1199.

I remember Professor Thornton relating to me a happening at a lunch at which he was present when the great French scientist Pasteur was the guest of honour. The waiter set a plate before him, but, before he helped himself, instinctively and furtively he wiped the spotless shining surface of his plate with his napkin and then looking right and left to see if his action was observed. The microscope had revealed for him terrors where up to that time, no fear was, and he it was who taught us to know the germ as our enemy.

Here is a letter written from Clemency to my mother, written when she was perhaps ten years old, which illustrates my mother's relations with the children to whom she was always kindness itself.

'My dear Grannie, Please do you think you could send six plates and six pennie spoons and 2 penny knives, we should be glad if you could send them to us. It will not cost very

much. You see we want them for playing with in the tent when we play red indians and things. We shall want six more for when the cousins come, because some of the things gave us before have got lost, we will take great cair of the ones you are going to send us. If you do not send them to us we will have to take all the kitchen things, so you will send them to us, won't you, dear granny.

Please send them by return of post if you can.
From your loving Clemency.'

I have no doubt that they came by return of post.

Anthony, who was nine months old when we went to Benton, was by now full of activity and a very friendly person. A woman from the Whitefield Buildings opposite our house, used to come to us to char, and twice a week to bake bread, and he took to escaping from the garden, where he was perforce left a good deal to his own devices, and go across the road to visit her, or failing that, one of her neighbours, to be eventually brought back by them. The kindness they showed the child was very real, though the houses had a bad reputation. He looked on all with a friendly eye, and without exception they were all friendly in return and he was soon piloted safely back to his family.

The demands of the large and populous parish of Long Benton on us, and the work done by Diana in particular, will be best understood by reproducing an extract from the memoir written of Diana by Lady Laura Ridding which embodies what Diana told Mrs. Eden in her letters of the family and the parish happenings.

'Dec 15th, 1910. We have had dull dark rainy days; it is as if we lived under a heavy curtain. We are between Newcastle, Wallsend and Shields, and of course we get a lot of darkness and gloom, but it is healthy here and the gardens do very well, only most of our things get stolen before we get a chance of getting them ourselves. Last night our coachhouse door was broken open and coal stolen and the doors left wide open (the loss was of little consequence as we have 25 tons of coal a year supplied free by the colliery under the lease).'

'I must say that with few exceptions, people are most awfully nice to Arthur and I can't tell you how much kindness we get. Nothing could be kinder than the shopkeeping class—splendid families some of them are! The professional people, too, are awfully good.'

References to the children continually recur. 'Oliver never grumbles. Whatever I ask him to do, he is always ready to do it.' 'We got our dear Stephen back last night, big and strong and well and we hear that the school is "lovely", which sounds all right doesn't it.' 'He was so keen to rush upstairs and kiss and hug Romola. It was so delightful to see the delight of the babies at having "Tee Wee" home, as Anthony calls him.' ... She then continues, 'I really do want a change, as it is somewhat too strenuous here, and I haven't been very well. Just from having one thing on top of the other.'

'I want to know, if it isn't a bother, whether you would keep me the pretty papers and scraps off crackers this Christmas for a little boy of six in the slums opposite. He comes to my Fairy Tales (readings). His father is a miner, earning sometimes £2 a week, and mostly drinks it. His mother died a year ago and his elder brother some months ago of "A-pen-cyprus" (appendicitis). Now poor little Joe waits and waits for his father coming home at night. No supper—no nothing! Sometimes father comes all right—sometimes drunk— sometimes not at all and then the little fellow of six creeps supperless into the empty house and has to sleep by himself. I asked him if he was afraid. No! I baint afraid now! he said. A little old man of six with a dear little face.'

'March 6th, 1911.—We had a capital nursing class on Thursday evening. I do look forward to the nursing evening. I've been looking after a nine days old baby for two days and a night. Its mother was dying, poor soul, quite unconscious but with eyes wide open and such a dreadful look. She worried and worried when she was ill as to what would happen to the baby and six others. I only wish I could have let her know it would be looked after. She was unconscious three or four days through Bright's disease. Such a good woman, caretaker to our lay preacher. Well, I took the baby away, as it seemed so incongruous, the woman dying and the little baby, just beginning everything, lying beside her. I retired to another room here, and had a lively night with it. Most beautifully clean and nicely dressed. Meanwhile the poor woman died and I arranged to take the baby back last night, when there came a message, the other children had developed measles and the poor father, who was devoted to his wife and so sensible and good with the children, was ill. We have placed the baby with a nice woman. As she lives almost at the gates, she just runs in for the food, which I prepare all ready, several meals at a time for the child is fed every two hours. People have been very kind about the case.'

'March 27th, 1911. We have had a very busy time. The day before the Confirmation I met the governess out with the twin babies, (who came to stay with me last autumn, whilst their mother had a holiday, the first, I believe, for nearly three years). I asked how she was, and the governess told me that she was not very well, and was dreadfully worried, as the whole of the drains had to be relaid inside and outside the house. Imagine no water, no bath, open pits in the house, and four children, two of them Anthony's age. They were to begin next day, and they were in despair! To make a long story short, the governess and the two elder children and the baby twins migrated up here to the vicarage for a fortnight, and their poor mother was at once laid low with horrid influenza in their disgustingly drainy house. Miss X is a very nice Scotch girl and we like all the children and ours are delighted to have the companionship of them.'

In the evening they romped in these big rooms and hall ... The night that the Bishop had supper here, we were twenty four feeding in the house (all the food had been got ready by Diana.)

Another letter gives an account of the Coronation festivities on June 22nd 1911. Five hundred and sixty sat down to tea in the vicarage garden and the whole population freely walked in and out. 'Not one flower was picked and not one scrap of paper was left lying about. A few days afterwards, about twenty five old people were entertained in the drawing room with music, singing, roses, tea and quiet strolls in the garden. It will amuse you to know that the vicarage is spoken of as "the Public House of Benton", because so many people use it, but that's as it should be.'

A letter from my wife to a friend tells of the welfare of Brown Willy, who accompanied us in our migration from Cornwall. 'You will so like the owlies when you come to see us. Brown Willy has now a white wife—a barn-owl, whom Romola has called "White Woolly" which we think is a delightful name. The two owlies live in a hole in an old chimney in the corner of the garden wall. You can look down on it and see them. Brown Willy is as tame as ever to me, but he does not care to be touched by the rest of the family though he will not move, but if he hears a strange footstep ever so far off, he dives into the chimney hole at once. We hope for some baby owls later. Of course we have to put the old birds in an aviary now, as they would be stolen or killed by the pit lads at once if they got loose. In the awful frosts I brought Willy in at night as he had not quite made up his mind to live in the chimney, like White Woolly. Whenever he hears me speak in the house he utters a long answering tremulous hoot, and then his cheerful call note. Now the two cuddle in the hole together and I shall have to hurry to bring him in. An unemployed labourer has made me another aviary as I want to bring up two baby horned owls—the kind about here. I should like to collect all the English owls, mine are so tame, and in such splendid condition. The poulterer gives me all his poultry heads and odds and ends for them.'

In the year of the Agadir incident Stephen and Clemency accompanied me to Germany and Switzerland for a short holiday. We spent our first night at Crefield at the house of a silk manufacturer, whose daughter had stayed with us at Duloe, when Fraulein Ecklar, her friend, was with us as a mother's help. Fraulein Ecklar met us at Cologne and we proceeded up the Rhine by steamer for the greater part of our journey to Darmstadt.

'I never thought you would come! Don't you know that war has broken out?' was her greeting when we met. I questioned this, and she answered, 'We had a telegram from an officer at Metz this morning, asking us to take in his wife.' This was disturbing, but I did not believe that war had or would come. This time I was right. How innocent some of us were in those days!

So we went on to Darmstadt where her father was the manager of an important bank, and a few days later I proceeded to Switzerland with Stephen, and left Clemency at Darmstadt with the Ecklars.

Mrs. Eden had been a Swiss heiress and had married Mr. Morton Eden when he was at the Embassy in Berne; he had been dead for some years. Her Swiss home was at Merchlegen, a few miles from Berne on the Aar, a delightful place to stay in. Her English home was at Kingston, near Taunton. My wife's great friend Violet Eden, now Mrs. Street, was also at Merchlegen, where Diana had spent the happiest days of her early life. I could then talk to her of it with understanding.

We stayed again at Darmstadt on the way back, when we picked up Clemency and saw a little more of Germany. How like German family life seemed to be to the English! There were two girls and two boys, both of whom were killed in the first war, in this Darmstadt home.

Our friendship survived the war of 1914–18, but I wonder what the story is now. Fraulein Ecklar was a very clever well educated woman and we often discussed with her our relations with Germany. There was no hostility to England in her, but clearly a feeling that we, the most successful member of the Germanic family, had been lucky beyond our deserts.

I do not think that she held any articulated theory of Herrenvolk, but she was convinced of the greatness of Germany, and before the war felt an enthusiastic loyalty for the Kaiser. What a tragedy the history of the world is!

She stayed with us after the first war to our great pleasure. But we were never able to contact her after the second war—she had vanished.

Diana had not been well for some little time, and when I came home she saw our doctor, and by his advice, a specialist. The next time the doctor came to the house, I asked him as we walked to the gate—what is the real position? That anything beyond cure was the matter had not crossed my mind. He replied—she may live for four years.

Yet hope did not die immediately, she was young and very courageous. I see a note dated Tuesday April 14, 1912. 'This was our last good time together'—and I still had hope!

The doctor told us a little later that the northern winter was too cold for her, as it was essential that she should avoid chills and she elected to go to Looe. I think that she realised how serious the position was, but she gave no sign and busied herself in other things.

Our former parishioners at Duloe of all degrees came very frequently to see her, which gave her great pleasure and she was much touched by their kindness.

She had a wonderful gift for drawing birds and the seagulls on the estuary were a great source of interest to her. Her spirit was indomitable. She had Anthony and the two girls with her. Stephen and Oliver were at school.

Later she moved to Kingston close to the Quantocks to stay with her dear old friend, Mrs. Eden.

A great friend wrote of her that she was a most unselfish and sympathetic mother, meeting her children's little troubles with tender truthfulness. She was undoubtedly sometimes rather sharp and impatient with them. Once when Stephen was about eight, she told him she was afraid that she had been a very cross mother. To which Stephen replied, 'Never mind, Moutie, we know you do your best,' and she did.

She mothered the children herself, and nothing was too much trouble where the children were concerned.

A great friend said to her that 'children soon forget their mother. I was barely three when mine returned to India and I very soon lost all recollection of her.' Diana caught her up rather sharply. 'I hope they do. I think that it would be an awful thought that a baby is fretting for you.'

One of her strictest rules was that all the children should be treated alike with no favouritism whatever. 'I once received a reproof from her at Nottingham, when the twins were babies, by asking which was Arthur's favourite. I took good care never to sin like that again.' (from a letter written by Miss Couper)

I was for a short time alone at Long

Benton, but I had made it known to friends that we must return south. In the early spring I was offered by Colonel H. M. Ridley the living of Maperton, three miles from Wincanton in the Blackmore Vale district of Somerset.

Just before the 1912 strike took place an amusing incident occurred. A young Yorkshireman arrived to try his luck in Newcastle, and took a house at Long Benton, and became an interested member of the congregation. He was one of those men to whom business comes naturally. He knew by instinct what was saleable and what was unsaleable and proceeded at once to clear the lumber in his new shop which was cluttered up with hats. One day he asked if I would like to have some ladies' hats to sell for the benefit of the parish. 'All right, send them along,' I said, 'I will see what I can do with them.' The next day, when I arrived home for tea, I found our hall which was a good sized square room, filled to the ceiling with women's hats and our three maids absorbed in trying them on. I consoled myself with the reflection that at any rate they were burnable. For the next ten days or so our hall became a shop with the maids as saleswomen and the hats gradually disappearing at marvellous reductions in price. The maids loved the business, but I do not know what my wife would have said. We

173

got rid of them and thankful I was when they had gone, but the money taken did not help the church funds very much, though it was not too bad, but then of course we took no account of the maids' time. I think that they tried on every one of those hats themselves.

When my wife went south, my mother joined me for a time, and saved me from the added misery of a house left empty, which had once rung with the busy happy life of a family. While she stayed with me the strike of 1912 took place, which interested her much, and I have included some impressions and notes recorded by her of the strike. She had never been in contact with one before. The notes record her impressions.

'In 1912 there was a national stoppage in the coal trade. On February 27, Tuesday, we heard that all coal lying by the (pit)head of the Seaton Burn Colliery had been gathered up and sent away in trucks. Feb. 29th. Seaton Burn men left work today at 2.30 p.m. instead of 5 p.m. and no coal was taken up the shaft. The younger men all seemed very jaunty about it. As they were paid no wages they think the strike will not last long.

March 1st. The people still cheerful.

March 2nd. Old lime kilns and workshops are being converted into stables and the

174

ponies brought up out of the pit and having their shoes taken off. Miners are also provisioning their houses. Arthur and I went by train to Wallsend and by ferry on to Jarrow.

March 6th. So far the miners here seem to be enjoying a holiday, but Arthur heard this morning that some had been heard speaking very angrily on their return from a meeting held in Newcastle last night.

March 9th. Mr. Hardy (the curate) told Arthur that the miners had been discussing whether he is a wayleave owner or a royalty owner for he gets free coal from Seaton Burn colliery.

March 11th. Outside gas lights are reduced and people are warned to be careful of their consumption of coal in their houses. A parishioner told Arthur that on Saturday he took £30 less than usual in his shop, and a neighbour has come straight home today as he had only a 3/6 order by post. The posts are now to be reduced on account of the trains being so many fewer. The men in the shipbuilding yards are getting cross with the strikers. A dark red new railway carriage, moved by petrol, went past here yesterday. It was experimental.

March 15th. Today our local miners received their pay, and the consequence was that tipsy miners were in evidence, whichever way one turned. When a miner is taken on in these parts he is not paid until the end of three weeks, and then only a fortnight's pay is given him. So on striking three weeks' pay was paid them. In consequence they are not yet short of money. Our miners having thus had more money than usual to spend and the weather having been fine they are enjoying the holiday.

By now 720,410 are out of whom 327,000 belong to the North of England.

March 17th. As Arthur is going to Taunton tomorrow I insisted on a washtub of coal being secreted upstairs. Edith found today, hidden in the kitchen cupboard, a large lump of coal for Mrs R.'s attentive daughters to carry away. They constantly call here to see their mother. Mrs. R, the charwoman, says that the men are quite sure that the Government will buy the coal mines and that they will get all they want.

March 22nd. Bands of miners with flags have been parading the place this afternoon and eventually held a meeting at an old mine shaft called Billy Pit.

March 29th. The distress among the people opposite has caused us to get soup going, so that we may supply four of the families. People are adopting families to help with their scraps. But coal is not wanted by them, as they get it from the waste heaps. Arthur's wheelbarrow is being constantly borrowed for that purpose. He met a boy whom his companion asked what he had in his bag. The boy replied—"the minimum wage", when he looked in the bag there was nothing there.

April 2nd. The borrower of our wheelbarrow was much distressed because 100 men had had their names taken for fetching this coal, he being amongst the number. Four families, having, between them, 23 children now send here daily for soup.

April 4th. Walked with Arthur to see the people getting coal at the Old Benton Pit. Some had a hole to themselves. Some were having tea around a fire they had lit, but we were too late to see it crowded.

April 7th. In old days coal was not sold in Northumberland, and a great deal was used as ballast on the tramways. Large pieces were laid under the old waggon way. Four Byker hewers, who had heard of this, explored a claim, which they never left unoccupied.

Others were taken into the enterprise and the twenty partners realised twelve pounds a man in ten days. The dealers at Wallsend took all the small coal they could find at 3/- a load (15 cwt); the better coal at 21/- a ton. Other miners were stopped as they began undermining the tramway.

The river was by now packed with ships laid up until the day when they could get cargo. The railways were relatively idle.

Mrs. Randle (our charwoman, whose son was a miner) is still sure that the Government will buy the coal mines and that they will get all they want.

Meanwhile pawnbrokers' shops published the distress by the rows upon rows of mysterious bundles on their shelves—rising barometer of growing poverty. In the bundles were packed shirts and shawls, blankets and underclothing etc. The home fires had mostly ceased to burn and the clothing was passing from the owners into other hands.'

Cold and hunger stalked in the streets. However in the end peace returned and the days of misery were ended. Few of those, who did not live in the stricken districts, realise in any degree the horror of a prolonged strike.

We had many friends at Long Benton and they sent my wife a beautiful bracelet watch, towards which the children of the old village, our near neighbours, contributed their pennies. That especially gave Diana pleasure—more perhaps than anything else.

I found the months at Long Benton from the time she left very dreary, in spite of the presence of my mother and the kindness of everyone around. The large house deepened the sense of emptiness. I was thankful when the months came to an end. At last the day came to leave Long Benton for Kingston, near Taunton, where my wife and the children were living under the care of Mrs. and Miss Eden, her lifelong friends.

I shall never forget the journey and passing the familiar stations on the way. There was Durham and its Cathedral where I was ordained and where my visits to Dr. Greenwell created for me a picture of prehistoric man as embodying my ancestors. There was Darlington, near which lived a fine old cousin of my mother. She was a Miss Nesham. She had been a great huntress and on her eightieth birthday the hounds met at her house, and the Master put her on his horse and led her around the village. A little later she met a neighbour, a farmer, in trouble. He was taking exhibits to a show and there was a breakdown. She relieved the situation by taking charge of the bull and leading it on its very best behaviour to the station.

Then there was York and the part it played in my courtship with Diana.

One by one we passed them by, and towards evening crossed Sedgemoor. The sun was sinking and the light on the buttercups was glorious.

At Bridgewater a man got into my carriage and sat down on the seat opposite me. As we drew out of the station, he leaned forward and said—'Have you heard the terrible news?' 'No,' I replied, 'what is it?'

'The Titanic has struck an iceberg and nearly everyone has been drowned.' The Titanic was a giant ship on her first voyage and her builders had boasted that she was unsinkable. The sun seemed darkened and the glory of the evening light faded. At last I reached Kingston and as I approached the village I saw Diana with Clemency and the babes coming to meet me. Our separation was at an end.

The following is a vignette drawn by my wife which presents one aspect of our Long Benton neighbours.

A Jewel in its Setting

Outside the November rain poured down in a pitiless cold stream. A few smut covered trees seemed to lift their unlovely branches in mute appeal against their lot. The air was full of the distant ring of hammers in the shipbuilding yards on the river, which merged with the deep panting of a pit engine, but there was at least one cheery spot in so much desolation.

In the old coachhouse blazed a north country fire, a veritable furnace with glorious glowing masses of coal. The window panes ran with raindrops outside and with steam within. Over twenty children were crowded around the fire, and the damp rose in clouds from their pitifully wet garments. Everything else might be damp but the spirits of the children were not. It is little short of marvellous how the poorest children will laugh and sing under the most depressing conditions. To a stranger these children presented a deplorable sight. For the most part they were the children of parents who drank. Some bore on their bodies tokens of the quality of their homes, yet even big brothers, who had long outgrown meetings like this, were not unresponsive. When the lady who conducted it told them that it was unsporting to trample over the potatoes when they came into the garden to retrieve a football, they not only became more careful, but even kept the bed in order for the rest of the summer.

The meeting, which was presided over by the parson's wife, was held for children over six and under fourteen on Saturday afternoons in the winter months. The rules

181

for admittance were to wear a clean pinny and to bring a pocket handkerchief or a rag which would answer the same purpose. These children should not have been poor. Their fathers for the most part were miners, but the rags revealed the old story of parents, who drank and gambled during prosperous times, and in bad times their families went short.

The parson's wife had a new scheme. When the children were tired of mounting the table and reciting their time honoured pieces, she planned to read them a fairy tale. In turn children, with arms like sticks of rhubarb and chapped hands, got up and recited. Then when the slapping and stamping followed, the parson's wife would make some ragged boy hand down the child from the old table, happy and proud for the moment as any Prima Donna, and no one would remind her that it was the same piece we had all heard again and again for weeks and weeks past. Anyway this Saturday there were to be fairy tales after the recitations. But here our parson's wife had counted on too much. Certain it is that the time honoured ones of Bluebeard and such like evoked little interest 'Oh! we know that, it's in our Reader.' 'Teacher learned us that for dictation.' Then the parson's wife made a bold venture and began 'The Swan Brother.' The failure was complete. Did I say complete? I was wrong. Sitting a little apart from the rest was a child of eleven years old. I think I ought to have asked the parson's wife to describe her appearance, but at least I will try. To begin with, one was at first struck with amazement at finding such a type among other children. The dirty old shawl was drawn north country wise round a face of exquisite beauty. There was something of the Madonna about it, but the oval was not too soft; a rather low white forehead, round which strayed vine-tendril-like curls, with rather more of a silvery sheen on them than of gold. The eyebrows were slightly darker, and were drawn with the finest touch. And those eyes! A dark iris surrounded by quite a narrow band of grey, which was again outlined in black. Her eyelashes were dark, and the bluish rings underneath her eyes, and the faint blue veins on her temples, all told of her delicacy. A straight finely cut nose, a mouth with such a pathetic look that it brought the stinging tears to one's eyes, completed the face of Mary. No nickname shall be given her.

From the time that the parson's wife began to read, that child sat as if in a trance. She leant forward so that her tendril curls, now dried by the warm air, drifted in a tangled mass across her white forehead. Gradually the delicate little fingers that held together her shawl, let go their hold. The edges of it fell apart, showing the rags beneath, and the white neck supporting that fair flowerlike head. The child seemed completely lost. Her mouth was slightly open, and her breath came fast and short. Her companions were fairly romping now, but the voice of the parson's wife rose above the tumult.

It was too much. Mary was now holding on to the seat of her chair. The great tears were welling up and overflowing her wonderful eyes. Her lips quivered and drooped and great heaving sobs shook her slight little body.

'Did you like it Mary?' the parson's wife gently questioned, as the rest of the children with deafening noise pushed and clattered down the old stairs. The child could not answer but simply raised her eyes still blurred with tears.

Now, if this were a nice little Sunday School tale I should be able to tell you that Mary was the only child of a poor widow who by strenuous efforts kept her little daughter sheltered and pure among so much of the reverse. Instead of which I will tell you the facts. Three years previously the miserable child had been the victim of a criminal assault by her brother—a brutal young pit lad. This was known too late for the law to take action, though there is no less need of praise due to the Society, which did its utmost to bring the young brute to justice. Then occurred one of those things which are to me ever inexplicable. Even the respectable mothers in the buildings, who did care for their children, joined one and all in trying to make it easy for the lad to slip away. 'If t'wer my own lad,' they said—and poor little Mary, was she not someone's lass? But 'tis ever so. Women of all classes will act unfairly against their lasses for the sake of their lads. Imagine what all that meant morally as well as physically! Mary was for the time being the centre of attention in that filthy courtyard with its lounging inhabitants at the open doors, their coarse jokes, the filthy talk; the back to back homes with their greasy broken down banisters; the loathsome yard with its stagnant puddles, and bits of cabbage stalks; the row of three privies for both sexes right in the middle of the yard; the loathsome banter as young and old women discussed the event loudly, when they passed to and from these places! Was not all this enough to damn the child eternally?

And her parents? Almost any day, when he was on night shift, you could see the man, who was called her father (though I have no doubt he was not), a sodden stubby faced brute with blood shot eyes and with coarse hanging lips, standing at the outlet of the passage, smoking his short clay pipe, which he only removed from his mouth to spit. Every hour or so he would lounge across to 'The Green Dragon'.

His wife was a deplorably coarse looking fair haired woman, with a revolting light playful manner, a straight yellow fringe and pretty complexion. She would also make many a pilgrimage of the same kind as he. When he had the drink in him, her husband was a devil incarnate, and if his woman was terrified of him then, what of Mary?

The parson's wife appealed to me to see what could be done for Mary. We went across one morning to her home. The door was opened by a strange woman, only partially clothed, who was recovering from a debauch, looked out and laconically answered—'Them's flitted,' and then left us staring at the blank door. Nor could we ever trace the family. Poor Mary!

CHAPTER TEN

MAPERTON

On May 21st we left for Maperton. The journey seemed endless, for with every mile Diana grew more weary. Yet the distance was not great. The line of the Quantocks beyond Kingston on a clear day is visible from Maperton churchyard.

Maperton and its rectory were then an almost ideal place for children, and much of my time was spent in teaching and looking after them. They made great friends with our neighbours in farm and cottage alike, and used to wander off on their own account to pay them visits. The population of course was very small.

I made lessons as practical as possible. We began Geography on the 6 inch Ordnance Survey map of the district. First the rectory and our surround, then Maperton House and the little group of cottages nearby. Next we took it for a guide in walks, until they could lead me by the map to as difficult a mark as a marl pit as yet unvisited by them in a distant field. Next the basis of their lessons was their journey from Cornwall to Northumberland and from Northumberland to Maperton. The children loved Maperton. The Lawrences came for their holidays as before and the Homfrays were commonly of the party. It was real country life. The house was of two portions, an old one, which represented the earlier rectory, contained the kitchen quarters below and my study and two bedrooms upstairs. At right angles to it was a newer portion built in 1800.

In spite of illness Diana still had her triumphs. She had won a prize of £15 offered by 'Oxo' for the best design for an advertisement when we were still at Benton, and when she was at Maperton she followed it up by winning another prize, this time for £100. I remember vividly how she looked up from the paper as she stood by the study window and said, 'Look here; I am going to have this one hundred pounds.' It was offered for an illustrated advertisement by 'Tobralco'.

She made a set of plasticine models for first aid classes which were exhibited at the Bristol Health Exhibition in 1912 and were thus commented on by the British Journal of Nursing. 'There was a series, in plasticine, made by Mrs. Bax, who evidently knows her anatomy thoroughly, and must be an artist of high merit, and should have fortune in her finger tips. The wonderful examples of complicated fractures of the skull, of greenstick, comminuted, compound and impacted fractures of the leg, and dislocations of the shoulder and elbow, and of capillary, venous and arterial haemorrhage, must be seen to be appreciated.'

Twenty years before she had laboriously written and illustrated a book on bats. It was written in pencil in an exercise book bought at the village shop. The illustrations were drawn on white paper stolen from the chest of drawers in the spare room. She loved her Bat Book. Then one day the nurse in a temper (with someone else) threw it into the fire as 'des betises'. Now she would make a second attempt, and every illustration was drawn from live specimens of English bats in her own possession.

Some record of her early effort survives—'I remember as a child, a certain yawning hole on the side of a hill in Somerset. A few lichen-covered stones were roughly built around the opening and tradition had it that it was the entrance to a subterranean passage leading to an old castle in the neighbourhood. At all events it was a mysterious eerie looking cavity. Tall rank nettles grew thickly between the old stones, and brambles flung their thorny red stems and leaves from one side of the hole to the other. Into this horrid place I submitted myself to being lowered by a boy friend, and, I suppose, was fortunate ever to have got out of it again. What drop there was I do not know, but the sides were almost perpendicular and I found a resting place for one foot only. The earth and stones I had displaced clattered and echoed as they disappeared into the pitchy blackness beneath me; but above those noises arose the surging sounds of hundreds of bats' wings! They crowded round me and over me to such an extent, that, with my one disengaged hand, I picked enough off myself and the rocky side of the hole to fill my pouchy sailor blouse. My other arm was stretched high above my head, and my wrist was gripped like a vice by my rather scared boy friend. I can remember to this day the uneven round of blue sky, the stones and brambles silhouetted against it, and the freckled face and the old jersey of my companion.

When at length after frightful exertions I emerged from the hole and pantingly retired to some tall bracken a few yards away, we sat down to examine our catch. I remember they were all without exception horseshoe bats, but which kind I cannot remember.'

At first Diana seemed to be better for the change and for getting back into a home of our own in such typically Somerset surroundings, for Somerset was the county she always loved best. Then came catastrophe.

I had been in London for the day on business and arrived home in the early evening. As I entered the garden I saw Diana standing at the front door as though anxiously waiting for me. As I drew near, although, owing to my short sight, I could not see her face, her carriage betrayed that something was wrong. She was drooping as if her strength had failed. I hurried forward and as I reached her, she said simply, 'Louise is dead.' Lady Lawrence, her elder sister, to whom she was deeply attached, had been thrown from a dogcart and killed instantaneously the day before at Karachi in India. It was at Karachi, where Sir Henry Lawrence then lived, as Collector in Sind, of which he later became Commissioner.

This has been said of Louise Lawrence: 'Her monument in stone upon her grave in the shape of those tombs of the Mussalmen races, which she loved will be for the eyes of the people, who need a thing visible for their veneration. But her true monument is her work. And to commemorate her work in Sind and to perpetuate her ideal, the Sindhi community itself is organising in her name a society of women nurses, which will, it is hoped, by labour among sick women and men in every district, hand down a living memory and tradition of her spirit; and never suffer to be forgotten in Sind the name of her who was for Sindhi, and always must be while memory lasts the great Memsahib.'

And a senior Sindhi official spoke to Henry thus: 'Sahib, when I learnt of the death of the Memsahib, then was I afflicted with great grief; in all the country of Sind there was no such other Memsahib.'

As I looked at Diana I knew that this was the end for her too. She died in the early morning of Advent Sunday, December 1, 1912.

One of Diana's oldest and best friends, wrote as follows, in a private record of their friendship. 'I had been speaking of her, saying what slight hope I felt that she would live much longer, and that I was going to write my usual fortnightly letter and I little thought that it was already too late. That night soon after I had gone to sleep, I saw someone standing by my bedside with her hands crossed on her breast. Her face was veiled so I did not see the features distinctly. The vision was so vivid that I started awake. My first sleepy word was, so far as I am aware "Mother", but no sooner had I got full possession of my senses than my thoughts flew to Diana. They were seldom far off from her, nor are they now. I was not frightened; my feeling was rather one of annoyance at having to go to sleep again. When the next morning we heard from a mutual friend, who was living near the Napiers, that she was very ill and unconscious and that Rosamond (her younger sister, now Lady Lawrence) had been sent for, I felt sure it was already over, and was quite prepared for the telegram received a few hours later, announcing her death.'

She was laid to rest in Maperton churchyard on Wednesday December 3rd, 1912. The funeral was taken by Willy Paine.

'So passed away,' the friend continued, 'one of the most interesting personalities I have ever known. I feel more grateful than I can express for her and for Louise's most true and helpful friendship of so many years standing. We, who love Diana so dearly, can only rejoice for her sake, that the months of weariness and great suffering, so bravely borne, are ended, but how we miss her! Some years before, on hearing of the death of a great friend of ours, Diana wrote to me and said, "Well, it is something to be worth missing."'

Diana was a wonderful mother, every one of her confinements were faced in thought for the child. She would never take an anaesthetic, but chose to suffer in full the pains of childbirth. She felt that it was in paying the full price of suffering for the child at its birth, that the claims of the child on its mother's love and sacrifice were realised. 'If you do not face that, you begin your life as a mother without realising the height and depth of sacrifice due from a mother for the child, to whom she has given birth.' She showed me once a torn handkerchief, which she had bitten on in the agony of parturition. 'If I felt occasion,' she said, 'I would show this to a son or a daughter that they might realise what I have been ready to suffer for their sake.'

My sister in law, Rosamond Napier, kept house for us for some months after the death of Diana, and was of great service to us all. She was younger than Diana, but like her sisters, is very gifted.

My parish duties at Maperton were happily light, and I was able to devote a great deal of time to the children. It was easy to know all my parishioners well and to keep in touch with them. All the boys of age were in the choir. Ringers were pretty regular at practice as well as on Sunday. The colonel gave us a skittle alley and I often joined the young fellows there and I opened a branch of the Church of England Men's Society, which met in my study, and was I think, popular. My wife in spite of ill health had instituted a meeting for women at the rectory, which lasted on under my mother. The people were very friendly and were something of a happy family.

Stephen and Oliver were at this time both at their prep schools. In the holidays George and Michael Lawrence came to us as before and Margaret Homfrey and her two small daughters, Jean and Clare, joined us at the rectory. After the war began she was parted from her husband, who was in the Marines, and from Jack, her eldest child, who had just passed into Woolwich and they lived with us for a time and then went into lodgings in North Cheriton parish, about a mile from us. Jack speedily passed into the Artillery, joined us when on leave, but was badly wounded at Cambrai, where he won his M.C. Thus we became one big family.

Colonel Ridley, the owner of Maperton

who lived at Maperton House across the road, was very kind but rather a quaint friend. He was a fine specimen of a man, but walked with a limp, owing to the unkindly action of an unfriendly Boer. He was an old Etonian with the faults and virtues of that famous school. He had for a time been at Christ Church, Oxford, and then passed into the 10th Hussars. Woe betide you if you inadvertently said the 7th. I think that he would have felt it less if you had proclaimed that he had been at Harrow. The Government, he felt, set their seal on the glory of the 10th when they made its former Colonel the Commander in Chief in France.

To Colonel Ridley had been given almost everything that people desire, a beautiful home, money, friends and relations, and a wife to whom he was devoted, and who made his welfare the care of her life, but fate had withheld from them what they so deeply coveted, the gift of children.

They were able to entertain Royalty, and he could give to the County Cricket Club an additional pavilion for their ground at Taunton, and yet, he and his wife had no direct heir. In his early days he himself had been a good cricketer and polo player.

Here at the rectory across the road would gather five young Baxes, two Lawrences, and three Homfrays. 'Mr. Box,' as he usually addressed me, 'I'll tell you what you ought to do with all those kids—you ought to put them in a water butt and drown them.'

Yet he hardly ever went for a suitable drive without some of them. 'Would two of the brats like to come with me? If so they must be across at the stable in ten minutes,' was a common message. Generally the little girls were chosen.

At times he was capable of making some ridiculous complaint. One day he brought to me Anthony, my youngest child, about six years old, with our garden boy, Willy, aged about thirteen, who preferred to be Anthony's nurse to weeding the vegetable bed. Anthony was towing a toy horse and cart with some grass in the cart. 'Look here,' said the colonel. 'I caught these boys taking my grass. The grass was growing in a gateway in the lane. They will not understand that that is my grass as much as the grass in the field.' 'What is your claim for compensation?' I asked him, on which he turned the conversation.

I suppose that something had upset him, but he was not often like that; these moods quickly passed.

Poor Willy! He became a ploughman under the County Council in the world war and died quite suddenly leaving a widow and a daughter. He had natural good manners and was a nice trustworthy young fellow to whom we were all much attached.

The colonel always had a great respect for my mother. She was quick and caustic in repartee, and feared no man.

Colonel Ridley was an enthusiastic lover of cricket and one of his first actions, on buying Maperton, was to create a really interesting and beautiful cricket ground in the park. It was quite a feat of engineering. At the top end he erected the pavilion, and on the lower side a shelter known as 'The Hencoop' where the lady visitors were penned. He then raised a village team which made fixtures with local teams; and, as at Duloe, we had fixtures with stronger teams in which his guests took part: regimental officers from Salisbury Plain, battleship officers from Weymouth, and even the Somerset Stragglers. In these matches the colonel's desire was not victory so much as a close game. I took part in both sets of fixtures. Although my bowling days were over I was still a useful bat, who did not mind going in first, and was also useful at fielding at point, where I could see. The colonel himself, owing to his wooden leg, never played but always umpired.

The match which stands out beyond all others in my recollections was one with the Eighteenth Hussars in 1914 on the Saturday before they went to France. We hardly expected them to come, but as they said—they were ready to start at a moment's notice, and they could be back in barracks on the Plain in an hour from Maperton and it was far pleasanter to come and play than hang about doing nothing. We had played them twice before and they were like old friends.

I have no doubt that they were right. In spite of the glorious summer day, the beauty of the surroundings and an excellent lunch under the great plane tree in the house garden, it was like no other day I have lived through. We could not hear 'the cannon's opening roar' but away there in Belgium once more it had begun and before many days were over some of our friends were dead and their regiment badly cut up. Yet, I am sure that it was better to play in those long hours of waiting.

One day the colonel looked in with a book in his hand. 'I want you, if you will,' he said, 'to allow your name to be put on a card recommending my head gardener's sister for a Home. Here is a list of the voters for the Charity, and I want you to look through it and see if there is anyone whose votes you can get for her,' and he chucked a volume in which their names were recorded to me. I opened it casually and my eye fell on the entry of the name Ridley Bax. 'What a coincidence,' I said, 'Your name is Ridley and mine is Bax, and here is a Mr. Ridley Bax who has eleven votes. On the score of the coincidence I shall ask him for them.' My application bore fruit. We received a most friendly reply. He had promised his eleven votes already but he would buy eleven more and give them to our candidate, and would I come and see him? He was interested in genealogy, and had a great collection of papers connected with the name Bax. Perhaps I would like to come and have a look at them? I went to see him in London and in spite of the wartime trains had a very interesting day. I was shown into a very large room with a platform and on it a grand piano at one end and four chairs in front of the fire at the other. After lunch he took me up to see his collection. They were piled on a round table in another big room, above the room in which I was received. 'Look at any you like,' he said. I casually picked up one. It was my father's will. He died as a young post captain, just over 40 years of age, in command of a ship, in which he was then surveying Korean waters. His charts were still in use during the Second World War. The will itself was a very poor show. Mr. Ridley Bax asked me to come again and I should have much liked to do so, but with home ties I was not able to do so very soon—unhappily, for he died shortly after. To Mr. Clifford Bax however I owe the gift of some papers connected with our family, thanks to the suggestion of Mr.

Thistlethwaite, a friend of ours in Birmingham. Since I have retired I have with their help traced our direct descent before the 14th century and hope to go further back. This occupation passed with increasing interest many otherwise dreary hours and, besides teaching me their story, has taught me far more social history than I should otherwise have acquired.

Colonel Ridley had a considerable understanding of men and for him they fell into two classes—Gents and Not Gents. This classification had nothing whatever to do with social class or possessions. The Gents were people who were straight, decent and friendly, whose word could be trusted and whose life was inspired by active goodwill to their neighbours. The Not Gent was the man who lacked those qualities, whose word could not be trusted and whose goodwill was apt to fail.

Sometimes I think our neighbours wondered how we all packed into the house. If the weather was fine in the long summer holidays, and the colonel had looked into the angles behind our home, where an ancient mulberry tree was the centre piece of a small garden, he would have seen the whole troop of children sleeping in hammocks or on mattresses under its shelter the profound sleep of happy childhood.

The colonel often paid us visits. I can see

him before me now, clad in sports coat and grey flannel trousers and wearing a Homburg hat. He was always followed by a dyspeptic Scotch terrier of pampered appetite and uncertain temper. If he was going his rounds in the late summer, he would carry a long billhook and wage war on old man's beard, to which he had a great antipathy.

He would take the children for a ride in his car and not infrequently the way was enlivened by an incident. One day when it was raining, they passed an old stone breaker, working in the rain without an overcoat. When they returned an hour or so later, the colonel picked up a new mackintosh, which he had bought in Wincanton, and without stopping or saying a word threw it to him. That was quite a characteristic action.

The scene of another incident was the hunting field; there was a long wait by a cover. Some onlookers collected and the colonel was amusing himself by looking around. Among them was an old woman, who attracted his attention. After an opening greeting, he remarked—'You want some new teeth.' 'I have no money to buy them with,' she replied. 'Oh, that's the matter is it.' Then he took a card from his card case, and wrote on it, 'Please furnish bearer with a new set of teeth and send the bill to me. H. M. Ridley.' He put below the order the name and address of his dentist. 'Take that to my dentist and make him give you a set of teeth. He'll soon put you right.'

He used to keep a stock of clothes and boots at Maperton House, and many a gift went to dwellers in the parish.

The most notable case that I remember was that of a large family, partly made up of seven sisters. They used to appear regularly in church. To one of these he gave a blue cloak with a scarlet lining. The next Sunday was wet and she was the only one of the family in church. 'Where are the others?' asked the colonel. 'They bided at home as it is wet and they have no cloaks,' was the answer. The next Sunday all seven appeared in church in blue cloaks with a red lining.

An early lesson for the children was to ride a bicycle, and the process brought Colonel Ridley around with a real grievance. I had bought five second hand women's bicycles for 20s each and after giving the children a lesson in the garden took them up the hill past the stables and told them to ride down it. It was a grand place for learning—an easy start down a hill, a safe crossing of a cross road, for their road was on top of a ridge, approached on both sides up a steep hill. Then a turn at nearly 45 degrees into the rectory garden, where the bicycle could be left to come to a halt by itself.

The process of learning brought dear old

Colonel Ridley around to make a strong protest. 'We can't take the horses out of the stable yard because of your kids' damned bicycles. Tell them to stop.' I explained the situation and told the children to wait until the horses were safely away. 'In an hour or two they will have learned to ride and will never want to do this again,' I told the colonel.

As soon as the children could ride a bicycle with confidence, expeditions became the order of the day. The country around Maperton is full of interest. Our first expedition was a midnight picnic on Cadbury Castle when the moon was full. It appealed to the sense of adventure for the hill is full of legend and history, and is said to have been a stronghold of King Arthur. Cadbury Castle is called Leland Camalotte, and there I introduced them to the Arthurian legend.

Our next expedition was to Glastonbury, Wells and Cheddar. Very appropriately the foreman of a small brickworks in the parish gave me, not long before we went, some strange bones found in the clay which they were digging for material for bricks. I sent them up to the British Museum for identification. They proved to be portions of the fin of an ichtheosaurus. That was a good opening for discussing the past history of Sedgemoor as we sat on the top of

Glastonbury Tor a few days later. There was also the Glastonbury legend to tell.

Our first bigger expedition was in Wilts and Dorset, staying away two nights, and was across Salisbury Plain from Lavington via Stonehenge and from there to Dorchester and Maiden Castle. I am now amazed at my courage. It was wartime. I took with me five young children and as a matter of principle made no arrangements. I wanted them to learn to move about with confidence and resource.

We were lucky in Salisbury, though one of my nephews reminds me that he got a scolding when we were looking at Salisbury Cathedral and I was pointing out some elementary facts about the wonderful building in front of us. On him my words were thrown away. The future engineer was immersed in the study of a traction engine, and I reproved him for not attending to what I was saying, when I ought to have recognised his natural instinct and foreseen his future. He has explained this to me since.

On our second day we set out for Blandford early. The sun had risen in full glory and there was plenty that was of interest to see on the way. We visited anything that attracted our notice and our meals were prolonged. At 6 p.m. we were miles short of Blandford; the day was changing and a bicycle had broken down.

Ere long a light rain began to fall. I took Oliver, the smallest of the party, up behind me and George Lawrence, the eldest and biggest of my flock trundled beside him the maimed bicycle. It was 8 p.m. and growing dark when we entered Blandford. It was wartime and there was no room in any hotel.

I asked a policeman for a suggestion. 'There's a pub up there, which might take you in,' he said, pointing to a bye street. I had a look at it. It did not seem inviting. I turned back and asked the friendly policeman for another suggestion. 'Did you try that pub?' he said, and added severely, 'I tell you that it is all right.' It proved to be a friendly little place, where they gave us a good supper and breakfast, and it was very quiet. But when I inspected the beds, I had to issue strict injunctions that the children were on no account to get into them, but to sleep in their clothes on their mackintoshes, spread on the beds.

The next day we were joined at Dorchester by my sister with Jean and Clare, her daughters, and Romola, and we paid together a visit to Maiden Castle. I think that the family enjoyed these trips as much as I did.

The war brought us employment in haymaking and harvesting. Actually our haymaking began before the war broke out. As I was returning for tea one afternoon from visiting in the summer of 1913, I found an old couple struggling rather helplessly to save a small field of hay. I told them I should return shortly and bring some helpers. The children fell into the idea at once, bolted their tea, and were speedily on their way, and soon everyone was at work. It is wonderful what children can do. When interested, they work with a will, and will attack anything. The small field was cleared and the rick built in a very short time.

On the next occasion in the same year a small farmer and his family were all ill together. They found us a boy with a horse-rake, and that was all the assistance we had or wanted. It was then that I built my first rick, unaided, but I knew that I must build up the corners. It did not look too bad.

The children simply loved haymaking and harvesting and made a very good job of it. For myself, I am sure, that it brought me nearer to my parishioners. We worked together and we often had our meals together. One labourer, who used to eat his midday meal with me, while we rested in the hay or in the cornfield, was later for years the trusted churchwarden of the parish.

I shall never forget a harvest scene in a big field at the bottom of a valley, along which on the hillside ran the high road to Plymouth and the West. The farmer and his men had gone away to milk and we were carrying on.

My eldest daughter in a blue dress was standing on the load receiving and packing the sheaves. Her golden hair was blowing out in the light breeze. Two boys in O.T.C. khaki were helping to get the sheaves up. A child was leading the horse, and two or three small ones were playing about. A convoy passed along the road above. The soldiers cheered and waved to us and we answered ecstatically in the same way.

There was in the air a sense of urgency, for the rooks were circling around the elms, which was interpreted locally as a sign of rain, and very soon the plough should be at work again, and the great field, shorn of its crown of glory, be turned up once more, except where the trifolium patch was already four inches high.

I have on my writing table an antique silver box most attractively embossed. Within are the names of the farmers whom we helped. It was given to me when I left Maperton, as a remembrance of those days of harvesting and haymaking together. It then contained a roll of notes, but alas, unlike the box, those notes soon disappeared. However I greatly value the silver box and from time to time reread the names and enjoy the picture they conjure up.

The names engraved within it are J. Crees, E. J. Day, J. W. Hansford, L. Hunt, L. de Las Casas, D. de Las Casas, W. H. Perry,

W. J. Rideout. June 1917.

It was then that we discovered another form of harvest. Colonel Ridley had arranged for a cut of trees in a small wood called the Knapps, half a mile away on the hillside. The tops had been left where they fell. Coal was very expensive and scarce in the village, so I asked for them, a request Colonel Ridley gladly granted. Then I arranged village picnics to collect the spoil, and the women, children and old men came. Autumn was drawing on, and we would gather at midday and again at tea time before they went home, around a great fire of waste wood, beside a little stream from which we filled a great kettle. Even my old mother used to attend. Those days became a cherished memory with us all. Years after, whenever we met again, we would recall them, the rhythmic noise of the saw, the ring of the axe, the sharp crack of breaking sticks and above all the cheery voices of women, old men and children. How beautiful those recollections are!

'Loading faggots' I found to be a different matter. 'Who would fardels bear?' They are heavy and I had not learned the knack. One day we nearly had an accident. The waggon had been loaded high in the wood, where the ground sloped. We were on the side of a hill. When we moved the waggon, it began to slide down the hill sideways. Just beyond it the slope steepened and if we reached that, a capsize was inevitable. Colonel Ridley, who had paid us a visit, fairly danced in his agitation. One more foot and there would be catastrophe. I have never seen a heavily loaded waggon capsize, but then that disaster seemed inevitable. At the last moment our very skilful carter got it moving in the right direction and slowly we drew it into safety.

What a help to our neighbours this wood was in those difficult days. How they enjoyed those picnics and loved to talk of them in after years!

I received some other marks of appreciation, the strangest of all was the offering by a very old neighbour, whose garden I had dug. 'I want to give you something,' she said, 'for all that you have done for me. It seemed I had nothing to give but a thought has come to me.' Would I accept the contents of her earth closet for my allotment? I told her that I could not think of taking advantage of her most kind offer. I should be robbing her garden!

The children learned quickly to help in the garden. Here was our method of planting potatoes. Clemency and I moved the line as required. I dug the shallow trench. Clemency with a stick measured the distance to the spot where Romola should place the seed potato. Anthony attended her with a tray of seed potatoes. Jean sprinkled guano. Oliver followed with a rake and covered in the seed. In this fashion we worked co-operatively and the work was quickly done.

In the bitter winter of 1914–15 I used to get up early as soon as it was light and go out and turn up with a crossaxe slabs of frozen earth. When the thaw came it used to go down beautifully as I raked it out. How I enjoyed my cup of tea and bath after my early spell of hard exercise. A crossaxe, under the right conditions, is a most satisfactory weapon.

Even the games we played were devised to make the children use their wits. One of the best was 'Submarines and Foodships'.

The rectory could be approached through a big front garden, an orchard or a field. The front door was the port. Submarines were forbidden to cruise within carefully defined lines, but might pursue to the front door. The food ships might use any ruse they could think of. Each foodship carried a sweet. If they brought it to port, it was theirs to eat; if they were captured, the submarines ate the sweet.

Thus while we played, two women appeared bringing in the basket of clean linen. The submarines failed to challenge. Ten yards from our front door, the women put the basket down, turned it over, and out scrambled a small foodship, who rushing to the front door, the port, was then licensed to consume his cargo, a sweet. Another time a clergyman and his wife arrived to pay a call, she carrying an open parasol. After the manner of children seeing callers, the watching submarines faded away, while the visitors advanced quietly till within ten yards of the front door, they then uttered a shout, threw away the parasol and ran into port with skirts and coattails flying. It was I and Clemency.

We played another game once on a still moonless night. We were divided into two parties, one headed by Henry Lawrence, then on leave, and the other by myself. Their part was to prevent anyone passing through the orchard from the field to the front garden. The defenders could throw their line of watchers anywhere in the central part of the orchard. Our part was to get through safely as many of our party as we could.

For a time nothing happened. The minutes passed slowly and the defender became a bit bored and sleepy. Then there were light footfalls. It was only a grazing horse that came through. Every now and then it lifted its head and advanced a few paces, zigzagging its way. However it was at least something for bored watchers to look at. In this way it passed through the line of the adversary.

Suddenly the horse giggled. The sound was most audible in the utter silence, and a voice shouted, 'Run for it.' There was a rattle of falling wood and the whole field was in quick motion, the watchers trying to atone for their carelessness and their opponents to make good their passage. Their only capture was the small giggler, who was towed by his father to the wire fence, but caught by the leg as he tried to get through.

The horse was very artistically made. Its head was a broom covered to look its part in the dark, and artistically worked to imitate feeding by my eldest daughter. The others of our party, suitably draped, and arranged, made up the body and legs.

When Colonel Digby of Sherborne Castle, the Master of the Blackmoor Vale, went to France with the Dorset Yeomanry, Colonel Ridley was elected to be Acting Master during his absence, and on one occasion at least he got me into great disgrace with my brother clergy. Inadvertently, he arranged a Meet for Ash Wednesday at Maperton House. I told him that I should not be there. In that case, he replied, 'I shall not attend your services.' We ended our discussion with a compromise. He would attend my services, and I would attend his Meet at 11 a.m. So he came at 10 a.m. and again at 7 p.m. to service and I attended his Meet at 11 a.m. Like most compromises this was much criticised. My critics were my brother clergy.

When Colonel Ridley became Acting Master of the Blackmoor Vale, he bought a donkey. When people asked why he bought it, he said it was to be a companion for the pony. When hunting began, a purpose appeared. The field had become very thin. The little girls should appear at Meets on it, and I ought to take them. Thus hunting began for them and for me, Anthony and Jean and then Clare were in succession in at the death and received a brush. Romola was unlucky, but one day the front door was opened and a brush was thrown to her. So all of them had a brush and what was more important had taken a first step in learning to ride. When we left he offered us the donkey, but I had to refuse it. These things were not compatible with work at Radstock.

On another occasion after the 10 a.m. Matins, which he and his dog came to normally every weekday morning, he halted as we walked down the path from the church together, and said, 'I want to ask you what you think I ought to do? I feel very upset about something. I have been up this last week to Chewton for a shoot. Waldegrave and I, you know, were in the same house together at Eton, and have been friends all our lives, and what do you think happened. He knows of course that I am now Acting Master of the Blackmoor Vale and what do you think he did? When the bag was laid out at the end of the shoot there was a fox laid out with it. Of course there is no hunting around Chewton, and in that sense it does not matter. If he had thrown it over the hedge I should simply have looked the other way and not seen it, but to lay it out with the bag was too bad! Everyone seemed to be looking at me and expecting me to say something. It was most awkward for me. I am very hurt about it. What would you do about it?' I commiserated with him, and said, 'I am going up to Chewton to stay there myself in a day or two, and I will talk to Lady Waldegrave about it.'

Even now I hear from time to time of exploits and adventures which occurred at Maperton during those years, of which I had not heard before. On one occasion Clemency, my eldest girl, who in some shadowy degree represented law and order, was the heroine. She had fallen out with the boys, and took refuge in her room where she locked herself in. The boys besieged her and the siege became a blockade. Clemency however was not idle. She made a rope of her blankets, and having secured this rope in some way to the leg of the bed, descended by it to the ground and went off to tend the garden, leaving them to blockade the empty room until they were sick of it. When on a second summons they came to tea, there she was at the table. Then the laugh was hers.

On another occasion Romola and Jean and Clare Homfray had been having tea with the Rideouts who lived in the adjacent farm. They were taken upstairs to the attic, and dressed up from some clothes stored there. They enjoyed dressing up very much. On the next occasion that they were bored, it happened to be early on a Monday morning, one of them suggested that they should steal up into the Rideouts' attic and repeat the dressing up. I am glad to say that they were caught and learned what the Rideouts thought of it. It did not breach their friendship, but they learned a lesson they never forgot, and I never heard of it until a short time ago. It was I think, very nice of the Rideouts not to tell me. They knew that I had my hands full.

In my day there was at Maperton a small school, staffed by a head mistress and pupil teacher. The head mistress was an influence for good right through the parish, and in its small way the school flourished. The elder children mostly went to North Cheriton a mile away. The walk did them no harm, any more than a similar walk, four times a day did me harm at their age. It taught me to walk. Now children are encouraged to lose their legs.

The little school has gone; the influence of the school teacher in the village community is no more. Parents seem to avoid a village where there is no infant school, and there are now hardly any children in Maperton which is a poor place compared with what it was, when it was full of young life.

The school teacher's name was Miss Prickett. It should be remembered with honour at Maperton, where she lived on for some years after retirement. My children remember her with deep affection.

The housemaid came to me one day and said—'There's a man at the door, who I think wants you but I cannot understand a word he says.' When he saw me he said, 'Do you remember me—Sussex Street?' He was an old neighbour of mine. His doctor had advised him to try to get down south as he was on the verge of consumption. He had worked his way in a boat to Southampton, but the tongue of the countryside was too strange for him. He could not understand the people nor they him. Now he was on his way back to Southampton, but he had learned where I was and had come to see me. He had heard of my troubles. I thought that he was probably in want of money—shame be to me! As delicately as I could, I offered him help. No, he would have none of it, me it was that he had come to see. After breakfast and a long talk, he went on his way, and that is the last I have seen of Sussex Street. The recollection of this incident fills me with the same humility as my farewell happening with Bill Tamblin at Duloe.

During those years I never lost faith in God's creation, and strange as it may seem to those critics who overlook the office of the poet as prophet or interpreter, Tennyson brought to me sometimes comfort and encouragement in poems which seem to be forgotten, 'The Making of Man', 'By an Evolutionist', 'The Silent Voices', 'Faith', 'Follow the Gleam' and the like, or in other moods the great religious poems of Browning, to whom Westcott introduced me, did the same. Later I came to love Wordsworth at his best. My mother taught me as a boy to hate poetry. It was in the slums of Sunderland that a genuine love of it began to develop, and that love began where it had something of encouragement or interpretation to say to me in a hard and very uncongenial life.

Poets have been more to me than theologians, but for me the poet without vision of the unseen and eternal is a contradiction in terms. The true poet must know in some measure the infinite eternal the soul of the universe.

There were times when my surroundings seemed to me to be intolerable. I can remember one such. I had been sent a bunch of Dartmoor Heather, and as I often used to do when I lay on the hillside on Dartmoor, I buried my face in it. The scent called up in striking vividness the scenes and sounds I loved—the pursued and pursing sunlight on the hills, the music of the stream rising and falling as the soft breeze rose or fell.

In 1917 the parish of Holton fell vacant. The poor old rector had long since been past work, and the church people mostly attended Maperton. By the desire of the parish I was asked to become rector of Holton, and to hold it in plurality with Maperton to which arrangement Colonel Ridley somewhat reluctantly gave consent. My notice of institution was already on the church door, when I was offered Radstock by Lord Waldegrave. Years before, Lady Waldegrave, who often stayed with her sister Lady Ridding at Thurgarton, had expressed a hope that had been reiterated more than once, that I should come to Radstock when opportunity served, and I had told the children that this little colliery centre might some day be their home, when we passed through Radstock in the train on our way to Bath. Now it came to pass. Maperton has been a refuge in a time of calamity to me, and to my five little children it was the home of their childhood. Partly through the hayfield and harvestfield and the wooding picnics, they had come to know my parishioners with a quite unusual intimacy, and Colonel and Mrs. Ridley's kindness had been unfailing.

I left Maperton on July 8, 1917, and on the 9th I was married to Mary, the elder daughter of Edwin Palmer, a former Archdeacon of Oxford, and sister of Edwin James Palmer, who was (like his father had been) a fellow of Balliol, and afterwards Bishop of Bombay. I had seen a good deal of Mary Palmer when I was at Thurgarton, and from time to time since at Chewton or when staying with Lady Laura Ridding at Wonston. We were married at St. Giles's Oxford and then spent a week on honeymoon at Tewksbury. She brought new happiness to me after the loneliness of the last five years and was a wonderful stepmother to my family. She helped me once more to expand in outlook and sympathy and my work both at Radstock and at Moseley owed more than I can express to her.

CHAPTER ELEVEN

THE GAY COUNTESS

In the year 1821 a baby girl was born in London of German Jewish parentage, whose fortunes by some whimsical decree of fate were to be intertwined with those of the

Radstock miner. She died fifty eight years later in 1879, and her body was carried for burial from London to Chewton Mendip, a village about eight miles from Radstock where was her best loved home. The tower of Chewton Mendip Church is one of the most lovely in Somerset, a county of beautiful church towers. It dominated a thinly populated district on those uplands of the Mendip Hills, a landmark in a lonely countryside. Probably few who pass the church at train speed in their cars, linger to see what manner of church it is, for it stands at some little distance from the road, but those who do so, if they are among those blessed ones to whom an ancient building can speak, will hardly regret the delay. They may have no knowledge of architecture, and but little of history, yet the grace of the tower may delay them for a space, but even if they enter the church they may miss much of its interest. Their eyes may rest upon the frith stool and probably it will mean nothing to them, for the old Mining Law has passed from remembrance. Yet the temporary refuge of the frith stool must at times have meant no less than life itself to some exhausted panting fugitive, who had tottered to its safety when death was hard at hand.

Those who walk around the church can scarcely miss a monument on the south wall of the side chapel. It bears in profile the likeness of a lady no longer in her first youth. The inscription tells in outline her strange story and gives expression to the beautiful and passionate love in which she was held by her fourth husband. She had a genius for matrimony. Other people have attained no doubt the questionable prize of four husbands, but few can have emerged from such a test, without a stain upon their character, and won such whole hearted love from her last spouse.

But let the inscription speak for itself:

SACRED to the MEMORY
of FRANCES,
COUNTESS WALDEGRAVE,
Daughter of Mr John Braham,

Born in London, January 4, 1821, died in London, July 5, 1879. She married first John James H. Waldegrave, Esq. of Navestock, in the County of Essex;
Secondly George Edward, 7th Earl Waldegrave;
Thirdly George G. Vernon Harcourt, Esq., M. P. of Nuneham Park;
Fourthly, Chichester S. P. Fortescue, M. P. afterwards Lord Carlingford.

Her brilliant gifts, her noble and beautiful character made her the centre of a wide and

worthy influence, and attracted to her
an extraordinary amount of friendship and
affection.
Owner for many years of the Waldegrave
estates,
in the County of Somerset, and elsewhere,
she made herself a much loved home at
Chewton Priory
in this parish, with him who inscribes on
these walls
her dear & honoured name.
The words, which kneeling here, she best
loved to use were
those of the Thanksgiving—'Almighty God,
Father of all mercies,
We thine unworthy servants do give Thee
humble and hearty thanks
for all thy goodness and loving kindness to
us, and to all men.

Her body rests, as she desired, in this
churchyard,
this memorial is placed here by Chichester,
Lord Carlingford,
the record of a great happiness and a great
sorrow,
and a token of unspeakable gratitude and
love.

'For where your treasure is, there will your
heart be also.'

In the churchyard, on the sunny side of the church, in a space railed off close to the south wall, lie the mortal remains of Frances, Countess Waldegrave and of Lord Carlingford & Claremont, Knight of St Patrick and Lord President of the Council and Lord Privy Seal in 1881.

'*He was a peaceful Irish patriot, an affectionate friend and a tender husband.*'
'*Blessed are they who hunger and thirst after righteousness.*'

Not far from the church, a little further up the road towards Wells, is Chewton Priory, where this romance was lived out. It has been long shut up, but passers by may catch a glimpse of the house as they go on their way from Chewton to Wells, and may recall the romance with which it is identified.

The story of the father of Frances, Countess Waldegrave is told in brief in the Dictionary of National Biography. He was a popular tenor singer of Drury Lane, a German Jew by race and was left an orphan early. At one time, it was said, he had been reduced to such sore straits that he was compelled to seek a living by selling pencils on the streets of London. While still a boy his voice, heard in the synagogue in Dukes Place, attracted the notice of a member of his own race who befriended him and gave him instruction in music and singing. At the age of 13 he made his first appearance at Covent Garden and later he achieved great success at Drury Lane. He continued to sing in public until he reached the age of seventy eight. His voice had a compass of nineteen notes with a falsetto extending from D to A in alto. It is said that the junction between the two voices was so admirably concealed that it could not be detected in an ascending and descending scale in chromatics. His detractors accused him of vulgarity, and a story of him says that on one occasion he had been singing in perfect artistic style to the Duke of Sussex. 'Why Braham,' said the Duke, 'don't you always sing like that?' 'If I did,' was the reply, 'I should not have the honour of entertaining your Royal Highness tonight.'

To this man was born in his forty seventh year a daughter who was given the name Frances. The little Jewess grew up beautiful and full of charm endowed with sterling graces of character.

At the age of eighteen she married John James Waldegrave of Navestock in the County of Essex. Left a widow a year later, she then married the seventh Earl Waldegrave whose right of succession to the title and estates of the family had been contested but without success. The litigation caused a breach in the Waldegrave gamily, and the entail to the estates was not renewed.

George Edward, seventh Earl Waldegrave, has been described as one of the most debauched and drunken rowdies of his day. One year of her life, Frances, now Countess Waldegrave, spent with him in Newgate prison, to which he had been consigned as a ring leader in a drunken fray that had ended in the death of a watchman. Six years after their marriage he died of dissipation on the anniversary of their wedding day. So Dudbrook, the ancient home of the Waldegraves, with the Essex property and the Somerset Estates, which included Radstock and its collieries, and also Strawberry Hill, the creation of Horace Walpole, all passed to the little Jewess, now Frances, Countess Waldegrave, who had two passions, one for building, and the other for cards.

Her third husband was George Harcourt, M.P. of Nuneham, whom she married in 1847, a year after the death of Lord Waldegrave. With this marriage she entered political circles, and with such success that cabinet meetings were, on more than one occasion, held at Strawberry Hill. Mr Harcourt was much older than his wife, but according to Edward Lear, the artist, who knew them both well, despite age and nature, their union was close and she did all possible to make his life happier, but there was a shadow, her extravagance.

The little Gothic Castle, fashioned by Horace Walpole at Strawberry Hill out of an earlier building, had fallen on evil days, and its great art collections had been sold in the time of her second husband, but the house, which had been restored is described by Edward Lear 'as the oddest prettiest thing you ever saw'. A comment also has survived, which is attributed to Lady Townshend, of a somewhat different nature, 'Lord God! Jesus! What a house! It is just such a house as a parson's where the children lie at the foot of the bed.' This was only one of the several building ventures of the 'Gay Countess'. Once more wax candles burned through the night to the small hours of the morning in the rooms of that famous house, and women's faces lost their charm as they calculated the value of the cards they held. Thus her great fortune melted steadily and debts began to accumulate and soon no doubt affecting the prosperity even of the Radstock mines.

Her friend, Edward Lear, the artist, who gave lessons in drawing to Queen Victoria and published a famous 'Book of Nonsense' which is said to have passed through twenty six editions, wrote to Chichester Fortescue on the eve of his marriage to the Gay Countess, 'Try your utmost to prevent her embarking again full sail in a London fashionable life, a million cardy surface existence' … 'She will always have enough first rate intimates to create more than sufficient society, and may be an A1 leader without the need of a multitude of followers.' Perhaps her taste for cards had been contracted during the year she spent with her second husband, Lord Waldegrave, in Newgate prison.

The marriage with Chichester Fortescue, her fourth husband proved a very happy one. He became Chief Secretary for Ireland in 1865. Their first visit to the theatre at Dublin was the occasion of the best known story of her brilliant flashes of wit. Someone in the audience called out which of your four husbands do you like best? Without any pause of hesitation she stood up and replied—'Why, the Irish one of course.' The theatre rang with applause.

For the rest of her life she devoted herself to the success of her husband's career, and to that of the Liberal party. Her house now became one of their chief meeting places.

If we wish to know something of the love that Lord Carlingford bore for his wife we should read and ponder again the inscription he composed for her tomb which has been already quoted. She died tragically in 1879 in their house in London whither she had been moved hastily from Chewton and left her husband for twenty years to mourn that

227

rich companionship that he had lost.

She was still remembered by old people in Radstock under the name of 'The Gay Countess' when I became rector in 1917. Radstock had more reasons than one to remember her.

In 1847, a year after the death of her second husband, when the lease of the Waldegrave collieries at Radstock fell in, the Gay Countess took over the management of the mines and for the future the colliery trucks bore on them the legend 'The Countess Waldegrave'. This was quite a new departure at that time for anyone of high social standing thus to proclaim their part in trade, as trade was then held in deep contempt. In this she did a public service.

The year in which she took over the management was a bad one, and the people of Radstock were nearly starved.

Moses Horler in his Recollections says that people with long families had scarcely anything to eat except potatoes and a little salt. One Saturday in the early spring they made an engagement together and marched around the village and then to Mid Somer Norton, visiting the shops and threatening to pull them down if the price of food was not lowered. He continues, 'I witnessed this myself and I remember that they came back into Radstock Market about two o'clock in the afternoon. There they met a butcher's

228

cart, coming with its usual supply of meat for the market. A rush was made for the cart, which they threw over, upsetting all the meat into the road, for they were starving and desperate men. One poor woman rushed frantically forward and seizing a piece of bacon, she made off with it as fast as she could run to Clandown ... On the following Monday a magistrate was called upon to read the Riot Act.

The latter part of the life of the Gay Countess was no doubt the happiest. It was her fourth marriage, which taught her what married life may mean. Marriage had already brought her social position, wealth, pleasure—now it brought her love. She and Lord Carlingford, her fourth husband, were lovers to the end. The house which is most truly associated with this supreme experience and prize, was Chewton Priory. Here was her real home—a building shaped largely by her own design. In 1868 she wrote in her journal—'We are groaning at having to leave this dear place tomorrow for hateful London. We have been immensely happy here in spite of all sorts of little worries—broken chilblains, Mendip mists, east winds, weak eyes etc.' She loved Chewton, for Chewton was a real home.

It now stands empty, while the memories which cling to it, fade. When you have looked at the monument to that great love recorded in the parish church of Chewton Mendip, obtain if you can, a glimpse of the house, where that love found its home.

From the life of the Gay Countess let us turn to that of the miner in the Radstock collieries, some seven miles from her favourite and much loved home at Chewton Mendip. The Radstock estate and its collieries had passed to her on the death of her second husband, the eighth Earl Waldegrave. He refused to renew the entail on the estates of the family, which should have secured the succession to the natural heir, the ninth Earl, for he could not forgive his legitimacy having been called in question, and contested in the House of Lords. So at his death these great estates passed into full ownership of his wife, the Gay Countess. Soon they were heavily mortgaged to pay her gambling debts.

That is a fact in the history of Radstock, which for years had grave consequences, unhappy for the nominal owner and only less so for the tenants of his estate. That is the background of the history of Radstock from the death of the eighth Earl.

There was living in the parish of Radstock, when I became rector, a very old man called Roberts, who was much respected by his neighbours. We soon became real friends. One day I asked him—'Would you like to live your life over again?' As he answered my

230

question his voice rose and shook strangely with passion—'Live my life over again! I would not live my life over again; it were nothing but cruelty in those days!'

John Roberts was born in 1838 or thereabouts and went to work when he was eight years old—that is approximately when the Gay Countess assumed the management of the Radstock collieries.

He told me the following, and may gay and charming young things, who in the most irresponsible way recklessly dissipate the wealth they have done nothing to create, read and ponder.

John Roberts at an age when in our day he would have been in an infant class in school, used at about four o'clock in the early morning to go to work at Middle Pit. The descent did not take long, and the days were past when he would have descended sitting on the knees of a man, whose leg was passed through a loop in a rope, to which they both clung. John Roberts, I presume, was lowered in the hudge, the chief danger of which arose from men jumping in as it was taking off.

His story then followed to a great extent the evidence placed before the 1842 Parliamentary Enquiry.

In 1842 a Parliamentary Enquiry was held into the conditions of labour in the coal mines of Somerset, where my friend was already at work in Middle Pit, and at the

Enquiry men and boys among his own comrades were called on to give evidence. Mr. William Ashman, the manager of the Radstock collieries, was among those summoned.

The mines, he said, were then worked by a company under a lease from Lord Waldegrave. The boys are taken into the coalworks at about eight years old, but not before this age at all regularly. Since he had had the management of the works, no child, he said, had been employed before he was eight years old. About half the whole number of the work people are under eighteen years of age.

George Parvad, a child witness, gave evidence. It is not cold or damp. He cannot read much or write, but is learning to read at the chapel school. He does not know of any of the little boys telling lies or stealing. He does not like biding up long, but wishes to go underground. George Parvad was evidently by nature a diplomatist.

In some of the coal mines of this district the regular hours of work are only from eight to ten in number, but more often they are from ten to twelve and occasionally they are prolonged to thirteen.

In this district it is the usual practice for the colliers to commence work very early in the morning, often at 4 a.m., but in some pits they do not begin until 6 a.m. and in very few not until between 6 and 7 a.m.

Meals. In some of the coal mines of North Somerset they sit down while in the pit, for half an hour to eat something in the middle of their work, but do not come up to the open air. But in most of the coal mines in this district it does not appear from the evidence, that any regular time is set apart for meals. It is merely stated by the managers that sufficient time is allowed. The children in general say they eat their food in the pit as they can.

Physical conditions. The miners are with few exceptions a strong robust set of men, and their children have such a trying ordeal to pass through that, on the Spartan principle, they must either sink under it or become hardy and enduring. They do not however long retain their full vigour and they exchange from coal breaking, which is the most trying kind of work, to the ordinary labour of clearing the ways and propping the roofs of the galleries. In some mines where fire damp prevails, their health is soon broken.

Its peculiar effects are asthma and tight breath.

CHAPTER TWELVE

RADSTOCK I

I had first seen Radstock from the train, when I was taking my family to Bath to visit the oculist and dentist. We lingered for a few moments in the mean little station, which serves the line from Bournemouth to Bath. It was obviously a colliery town and how drab it looked on that grey autumn day! Few of its inhabitants were on the platform. Had my youngest son got out of the train and walked its main road at the appropriate hour, he might have asked, as a party of London Country Holiday Fund Children once did, 'Why are there so many chimney sweeps in this town?'

'Perhaps we shall come to live here some day,' I said, half mischievously. I had been told more than once by Lady Laura Ridding that the living of Radstock would be offered to me, if it fell vacant. My family were incredulous and refused to take me seriously. The train moved on towards Bath and they forgot my words. I confess that the prospect seemed to me to be very unattractive. I little dreamed of the interest and happiness that awaited me there and of the friendships I was to make in a time that now was not far off.

In the days that were past Radstock must have been beautiful, for it nestles in a cup in the hills, where three valleys meet, and three little streams unite and go on their way singing, to join the Bristol Avon. Those were the days when the steep sides of the valleys were clothed in oak scrub, and the smoke of fires, kindled by charcoal burners, betrayed the leading industry of Radstock in a time long past. In those days no batches crept out from the hillsides, and trout still rejoiced to lie in wait for their dinner where the streams meet, and rose when fly were on the water. Then the beauty of the valleys could win the love of those who lived there for two of the hills are crowned by a tumulus of an earlier race, placed where the dead men had, I think, sometimes loved to linger to drink in the view below.

From the field in front of that village a ploughboy collected three hundred articles, which belonged to Roman days and brought them one evening to show to a little Literary Society which we had founded. (I myself have never found anything worthy of mention except a fossilized Portugese man of war, a shell fish, now found, I think in West Indian waters. My fossil was found on the side of Honeycomb Hill near Sherborne.) The list of rectors of Radstock began in the late thirteenth century, and the first name is Robert, Persona, 1297. The scratch dial on the wall of the church porch recorded the hour of Mass, when the sound of the warning bell spread through the valleys.

The little community of Yeoman and peasants drowsed through the ages until the latter half of the eighteenth century. It was then that they 'heard tell' of coal being found in nearby parishes. Yet the trance of Radstock persisted for a time, and a certain 'Gentleman' Salmon, who with his partner Hercules Harler, were leaders among the early Coal Adventures, declared that if ever coal were found at Radstock he 'would get to the top of Norton Tower and flee down'. The hour struck in 1763, when the 'Old Pit' was opened at Radstock, but there is no record to show that Gentleman Salmon kept his word. It was then that the spirit of a new age descended on Radstock.

The last great disturbance in Radstock was still a living memory when I first came to the parish. A very tall man of advanced years might then have been seen lounging almost any day in the open space, which hardly amounts to a square, in the centre of the little town. Here opposite each other are the two leading hotels—the Bell Hotel, and the Waldegrave Arms. His address was quiet and pleasant and he had established in his younger days a local reputation for mowing, for his sweep with his scythe was very wide, and he was sought after by the local farmers to help on the farm when the pits were idle or working short time in the summer months. But once in his life he had seen the inside of a jail for his part in a riot. As he was tempted by his wife we will call him Adam, and his wife we will call Eve.

It was the end of a contested election and a great crowd of miners had collected in Radstock to hear the declaration of the result of the poll. The miners were a body keenly interested in the fortunes of the Radical candidate, and were confident as to the result. The Conservative hopes rested upon the support of the electors in the country district.

Very thoughtlessly the Road Authority had had heaps of stone tipped in the square for breaking up, for which it was a good centre for distribution, and they, strangely enough, never thought of the election. Now it lay there ready to hand, and plenty of it conveniently broken up, close to the Bell Hotel, where the Conservative candidate had his headquarters.

There was dead silence when the moment came for the announcement of the result of the poll—the silence of a great crowd, which is more impressive than the sound of many voices! When the success of the Conservative candidate was declared a storm of booing arose. Adam was standing in the front of the crowd taking his part in the uproar, and Eve was by his side. She believed in deeds. For her, words were not enough. She stooped down, gathered some stones from the heap, which lay ready to hand, and thrusting them into Adam's hand, pointed at the hotel with her finger. In an evil moment he yielded to temptation and flung a well aimed stone. For a second there was uncanny silence, but the sound of shivered glass tinkling as it fell was maddening, and the example was contagious. When the Bell Hotel was no longer worth a shot, the crowd visited in turn the houses of all the leading Tories and did not rest while there was a pane of glass left in any Tory window. That was the last great riot in Radstock.

My first rector's warden, then a little boy was carried down into the cellars of the Bell for safety, and there he stayed trembling while the mob completed its work. Even in my day Radstock was still regarded with dislike and fear in Bath, and people could remember the tag which was common at one time, I was told, in advertisements for maids—'No Radstock girl need apply'. On the other hand in my day one Radstock family at least had found its way into the Royal Household. I remember one morning being stopped at the bottom of Wells Hill by a friend, who told me that he wished to introduce me to his uncle. His companion, both in figure and clothing, looked like

Edward VII returned to life. He told me that he was the keeper of the King's Gold Plate at Windsor Castle. He had heard that I had been at Windsor for a Meeting of the Auckland Brotherhood, at the Deanery and wished that he had known at the time, for he could have shown me many interesting things. He was not the only Radstock person who has found his way into the service of the Royal Family.

Our new rectory stood in the low lying centre of Radstock and the garden was sometimes seriously flooded, so deeply at times that the family could launch an old washing tub, which came from Duloe, on it, and make a voyage. At the bottom of the lawn was a summer house and a deep square pool in which my predecesor on suitable days used to plunge in the early morning. I was always afraid of a child being drowned there for the garden was much used. At last one day when I was in bed with influenza and there was a dance in the garden I heard voices crying out, as people cleared off—'Have you seen our little Betty?'— 'Betty, Betty where are you?' and no voice answered the repeated call. I was on the point of pulling on my trousers and dashing out to the pool when I heard a cry, 'Betty's alright.' 'She has gone on with Amy.' I had the pool filled up after that.

There were nearly two acres of garden, but

the kitchen garden, on sloping ground above the house, was not over big. The front garden lay low, little above stream level, but the water never entered the house. It was almost entirely lawn. At the far end was a small copse. When we went there it was bounded in front by the railway, but while we were there, a strip was taken from us for a new road between us and the railway. We had a tennis court at the far end skirted by old apple trees in line along the kitchen garden wall, and on the railway side by tall willows. Near the rectory house were two fine acacias and rambling roses and a herbacious bed nearby. A line of trees and shrubs screened us from the railway before the new road was made.

The oldest part of the rectory may well have dated from the Reformation and was at first perhaps no more than what for us were kitchen and scullery with the rooms above. The last enlargement had been made in the latter half of the nineteenth century. Altogether it was a large house with good rooms and suited us well, with plenty of space for five children and their friends and with a dining room big enough for parish purposes.

Our garden was of great service to us. There was a beautiful clump of great beech trees by the front gate, an ornament to Radstock centre, and in it was established a rookery. Their proceedings were sometimes of general interest. On one occasion a quarrel caused two pairs of rooks to build in some low trees by the railway signal box. To the great entertainment of the signalman one pair stole sticks from the bottom of their neighbours' nest, while the neighbour's wife was sitting, apparently unconscious of what was happening below. Would the eggs fall through the bottom of the nest? Children from the London Children's Country Holiday Fund were absorbed in their doings. A little girl, standing in the doorway of her hostess's house, who had just arrived, saw them planing down towards their nests in the evening as they returned home. She rushed in to her hostess crying, 'Come quickly, come quickly,' 'There are such a lot of little aeroplanes in the sky.'

One day there was a sad quarrel and some of our rooks migrated to trees close to the primitive methodist chapel, and my friends condoled with me on some of my rooks becoming Dissenters.

Twice we had great meetings in the garden. The first occasion was a memorial service. A tragic thing had happened. Our Labour candidate, an ex-Captain in the Army, who had started in the ranks and done excellently in the war and who was deservedly very popular, was killed in Northumberland in a motor accident. There was a general desire to have a memorial service in our district where he had many friends and followers, but no building would hold the crowds expected and which materialized. So by request the service was held in our garden. It was a wonderful gathering, and I think the service with its hymns was very impressive.

The second occasion was a visit from St Hilda's Band from South Shields, in the County of Durham, who had been the winners at the Crystal Palace that year, and were touring and visited Radstock. On that occasion I had been out visiting and on my return I could not get in at the gate on account of the crowd. I had to ask a neighbour to let me drop over his garden wall into our garden. It was a beautiful day and there were many people—even on the hill opposite, listening.

The need for a recreation ground in Radstock was urgent. When the men came back from the war, we had dances in the rectory garden once a fortnight in the summer. They were well attended and I think much enjoyed, and it was very remarkable how little the garden suffered. The lawn was very big and the portion set aside for dancing was moved each time. It lay low and was damp and the grass soon recovered.

Our chance to secure a recreation ground

came when the Waldegrave property in Radstock was sold. Then we bought a field, but at a great price. It was vested at first in a public utility company of which I was the chairman and the clerk of the Urban District Council was secretary. The matter was urgent for the young fellows were returning fast from the Army and there was nowhere for them to play football.

Our purchase was not a first class field, but the football pitch was good. The trouble is that there is a deep valley along one side, and on the other the pitch is rather close to gardens. Everyone agreed that it was not ideal, but no one has yet seen any possible way to a better. Radstock is a place of valleys and steep hills, and is a fairly built up district.

I discovered an unexpected advantage in the football pitch being so near the cottages. Old people, even the old ladies, as well as men, sit in their bedroom windows and as from a grand stand 'follow the football'. It certainly gave them a new interest.

The next great need was a grand stand. How were we to get one? It was regarded as essential to our gate money to have a place where spectators could sit in the dry when it rained. To meet the need we bought a 100 foot vehicle shed at Warminster and I went up on three successive days with a party of young fellows to take it down and pack it in trucks for transport to Radstock. They of course wanted their bit of fun, so they set me to draw nails. When we knocked off for dinner, they clustered around me and asked to see my hands. I held them up with a smile for their inspection. There was no blister. Bah! said our captain, 'You've done hard work before.' I had.

I doubted if they would welcome my presence, when they went off at 1 o'clock to get some food, so I sat down on the grass to eat my sandwiches. They noticed that I was not with them and stopped and for a moment whispered together. Then the boss came back and said—'We hope that you are coming with us. We like to have the shepherd with the sheep.' Such an invitation was not to be refused, so I joined them.

We had in our number skilled waggon builders with whose help and guidance the vehicle shed was re-erected and transformed into a grand stand on the recreation ground.

There was much debate as to which side of the field it should be placed, and the vote was given for the wrong side. Two years after in a great storm the roof was sent flying. However all is well now.

It was difficult to get enough pound shares taken up, but the Co-operative Society, always to the fore in good works, stood by us. Before I left Radstock we had reduced the debt considerably, and the shareholders agreed to give their pound shares to the Urban District Council and to have the ground conveyed to them. For years now Radstock has been able to field a good team.

Dr. Savage, who was then Medical Officer of Health for the County, with whom I was brought into contact in connection with anti venereal work, said to me, 'You will do better anti venereal work with your field than you ever will with your lectures.' Yet we had some good lecturers, notably Sir Francis Champneys, who spoke very plainly at a Sunday evening service on sexual questions, (rather a bold venture in those days), besides lecturing to the United Bible Classes of Radstock in our church in the afternoon. No one complained or reported me to the Bishop.

It was not long before I was swept into the life of Radstock. One day as I climbed Wells Hill, I met William Bird, who became a great friend of mine. He was the secretary of our branch of the Workers' Education Society, an ex miner, trades union official, and now relieving officer. He invited me to join the Workers' Educational Society and told me that the branch would welcome my doing so. He went on to explain frankly that the Society was absolutely democratic and that no precedence of any sort would be accorded me because I was rector. I accepted the invitation con amore. At the next election of the committee, Mr. William Campbell, then chairman, a master at Downside, retired. He had been an excellent chairman, and on his nomination, I took his place. The members included several people, who counted for something in the life of Radstock, and some of them were afterwards colleagues of mine on the Urban District Council. Later on, a successful University tutorial class was also developed.

A very interesting feature in the Society's programme were Summer Rambles, which I always enjoyed. 'The essence of a ramble is comradeship and education.' For them we sought specially qualified guidance. A naturalist might accompany us to tell us about birds; a geologist to take us to a quarry, or a clergyman to show us his church.

It was a memorable occasion when my wife and I had the pleasure of entertaining Mr. and Mrs. Reuben George to lunch, who came over from Swindon to accompany us on our first ramble. He began his working life in the Gloucester Waggon Works, and at the age of 23, through the loss of some fingers, had to begin life afresh as an insurance agent. In his early years he became conscious of having missed something, and he said to himself—'It's time Reuben that you began to study.' He attended some university extension lectures, and a visit to

Oxford, through the instrumentality of a summer school, he counted as the greatest spiritual experience of his life. All his best in life seemed to date from that experience, 'I knew now,' he said 'what life is for. I knew now that life is growth in understanding.' But Reuben George was one who gave as well as received. It occurred to him that the people of Swindon, now his home, ought to know something of the country about them, and of the remarkable men and women who had lived there.

In a characteristic talk, which he gave to us that afternoon on 'Unconvential approaches to education among the hills and hedgerows' he told us how he had first organised excursions under the name of 'Rambles' and would lead his company to some attractive villages where they might visit a shrine, (i.e. the home of some former inhabitant of real interest or mark), hear a talk, enjoy a tea together and return with the moon to their homes in Swindon. He has been called 'the Saintmaker' because he rediscovered beautiful lives which were connected with the neighbourhood. 'Think what the country can do for your soul,' he proclaimed. He quoted the remark of a poor charwoman—'I never knew before that the world is so beautiful.'

The organisation of a ramble presented no difficulty. Each person brought his or her own provisions, a screw of tea, a cup and 2d. The host provided hot water, milk, a shady lawn and a waste paper basket for the collection of debris. The 2d paid for milk and tip, and we found a ready welcome to gardens.

Our greatest expedition was to Ammerdown, where Lord and Lady Hylton made our visit a very great success. The pictures were of special interest to our party. I was aghast when I saw what we were in for when we set out. All Radstock seemed to be on the march for Ammerdown, but Lord and Lady Hylton rose to the occasion, and I am certain that the trouble they took, did much to sweeten social relations in our mining community.

My friend and sometimes churchwarden, Mr. Howard Coombs, and I started a Literary Society, which was probably unique in that it had no rules and no subscription. We met at Mr. Coombs's house, and some of my most pleasant evenings were spent at it. Picture a large comfortable tastefully furnished and well lighted room, filled with people, two or three of whom are lying on the hearth rug in front of the fire for lack of other accommodation. The audience are of all classes, but school teachers preponderate. The paper may be illustrated by picture or song. Sometimes it was of unusual interest. An outstanding one was a three weeks record taken from the diary of the Revd. John Skinner, rector of Camerton, at the beginning of the nineteenth century. It was given by Mr. Howard Coombs, and it led in due course to the publication of *The Journal of a Somerset Rector*, of which more later. Another was the visit of a young ploughman, whose work lay on a farm on the Fosseway, and who had, in the course of his ploughing, collected about 300 objects of Romano British times. I am glad to say that in the case of the ploughman it led to more appropriate work.

Thrilled by that wonderful book—*The Pageant of Greece* by Dr. Livingstone, I introduced it to the Society and, sketching in the background, I read extracts from Thucydides to illustrate what Athens stood for; the kind of men who made Athens great; the type of leader with which Democracy is safe; War and Party Spirit; Melos the great crime, and Syracuse and Retribution. I was asked to repeat the reading at our Co-operative Society's Literary Guild, where my audience was mainly representative of the pronounced and active Left. They fell on these tempting morsels with avidity. The evening concluded with a resolution calling on the Urban District Council to add the book to their Library. A friend came to me after the meeting with a flattering request. 'I have to give a lecture at a neighbouring village next week. I wonder if you would mind lending me your notes, and *The Pageant of Greece* and allow me to give your lecture.' So we sat down to the notes, and a map, and I worked at the background with him. He was a fluent speaker and a man of intelligence, and I daresay presented the material better than I did. I felt his request to be a great compliment.

My friend, Mr. Howard Coombs, had a great taste for art. Pained by the bare walls of the big room in the council offices, where the dances and larger meetings of Radstock took place, he offered to the Council a delightful collection of reproductions of great pictures of Italian, French and English Art. The gift was gratefully accepted, but there must have been some division of opinion, for when we next entered the Victoria Hall, they all hung in an unseemly rabble behind the platform. However, at the next meeting of the Council we obtained leave to arrange them ourselves, and a very great improvement they were to the room.

The population of Radstock was about four thousand people, but the place was of more importance than the number of its inhabitants. It was the centre of the Somerset coalfield. Here were the offices of the Waldegrave collieries and the house of the secretary of the Somerset Miners' Union. It was also the centre of a Co-operative

Society, which worked through the district of about 20,000 people, and of a branch of the Gloucester Wagon Works. It was possibly more purely industrial than any other parish in the West of England, but it was well staffed from the religious point of view. Besides the rector, there were a Wesleyan, a primitive methodist, and a United Methodist Minister resident in the place, and usually a Baptist. Downside also had a little church there, which was worked from the Abbey. I worked in close understanding and comradeship with all except the latter. We made occasionally joint efforts. Once we had a 'Copec' joint meeting, and once a year a big joint missionary meeting. On one occasion on some town question I sat as chairman at a joint meeting of the Church Council and the Free Church Council, but it was in our bible classes that we came into closest co-operation. We each had a big bible class. They were popular in a mining community. Ours met in our large dining room on Sunday afternoon. It began at 3 p.m. but members could come in and sit down at any time after our midday 'dinner' had been cleared away, and first arrivals had to help bring in chairs and arrange the room. In the summer they would walk in the garden until it was time to come in. In numbers we once or twice touched forty. My wife played the piano for the hymns.

Sometimes one of our cats would attend. I have seen one jump on to the back of a lad who was sitting forward and coil itself around his neck, where he remained without moving until it was time for the prayer. On one occasion a cat brought in a mouse and dissected it in public while everyone watched the process. The friendship between the cats and lads, most of whom worked below ground, was very wholesome. Only once was anything broken in the room, although there was a dresser of old blue china there, and in bad weather the members often came in early—as soon as the table was clear. The accident was acknowledged directly we entered the room. It was a pure accident—not ragging.

The nonconformist chapels each had a bible class and once a year each in turn had a general rally, when their classes met together and were addressed by an invited speaker. We at once joined in these rallies. Between us we had a fine muster of the youth of Radstock. I always made a great effort to get someone with special qualifications to address them, when it was our turn to hold the rally. Professor Leonard of Bristol University, a most popular speaker, came two or three times. My neighbour, the Revd. G. Hanney, the novelist, came once or twice. Once to the great pleasure of his wife, who was a devoted member of the Church of

England, I secured another of the Professors of Bristol University who had been lecturing to our W.E.A. He had had a remarkable career. Driven from Russia when little more than a boy, he had spent time at several of the universities of Europe before he arrived in England, where he became one of the Professors of Botany at Bristol. His address was much appreciated by his wife as well as the class. His colleagues after the event kept asking him where next he was to preach.

Then I thought the time had come to venture a further step in co-operation. After consultation with my church wardens and some other of my leading people to make sure that the congregation would be behind me, I determined to invite one of the nonconformist ministers to preach at our weekday Harvest Festival service, but I was careful to write to the Bishop first, not to ask for his permission which would perhaps embarrass him, but to inform him of our intention, so that he could not feel that we were doing anything behind his back. The result was a great disappointment to me. He replied that he would be greatly grieved if I did as I proposed. The letter was kindly in its expression and I replied that I was greatly disappointed, but that I should not act against his 'expressed wish', and I imagined that the matter was closed. A few weeks later I received a letter from the Bishop's secretary informing me that the Bishop desired to give part of his charge at Radstock. I was rather surprised as I had had difficulty in getting even a Confirmation.

The day came and as his charge drew towards its end, I was surprised to hear the question of a nonconformist speaking in church referred to and virtually forbidden. What I had treated as a matter for private consultation was made a matter for public pronouncement in Radstock which seemed to me most undesirable under the circumstances. When the Bishop had concluded his charge, I got up and said that although he disagreed with my proposed action, he would, I was sure, admit that I had shown a sense of discipline. I had told him privately what I intended to do, so as to give him a full opportunity to express an opinion and when it was adverse, I had respected it although greatly disappointed. But as he had brought this matter up in public in Radstock, I felt bound to say that I still believed that my proposed course of action was the right one, and that it was with great personal regret that I had conformed to his wish.

I sat down and for a short space there was an unpleasant silence and then we proceeded to the next subject.

Twenty five years have passed and I may now mention an incident which gave me great pleasure, and caused me also deep regret. One of the nonconformist ministers asked if he might come with me to Moseley as curate. I should have greatly welcomed it, but the difficulties were too great. The proposal was a great source of happiness to me, and I only wish that it had been possible. He would, I believe, have proved a most valuable colleague.

I doubt if there were a place in England at that time where relations were more cordial and co-operation between the different Christian bodies, more sincere and ready for advance. I believe too that the condition of Christianity today would have been far happier, if friendliness and co-operation had been generally encouraged by the Bishops. Had that been so by now it might be bearing the fruit that we all desire, and have resulted in a working co-operation in many a parish in England. How much easier is would be to meet some of the great troubles of today if only that had come to pass, and if the goal of reunion were appreciably nearer.

It was in this time of discouragement that I had the following experience.

A Sacrament on Kilmersdon Hill.

Soaked by the rain, and battered by the
 blast,
Despondent, weary, heavy both of heart

and foot,
I faced the storm.
A thornhedge climbed the hill upon my
    right,
The tiny buds scarce showed against
    the sky,
From every thorn a raindrop hung and
    dripped.

Then unexpectedly a wonder came to
    pass,
The clouds were rent, the setting sun
    shone through,
The hedge with fire burnt,
For every raindrop in that golden light
Glowed like a lamp,
                            O World Invisible!

And as I looked, and marvelled, there
    arose a storncock's song,
Perched on the highest branch of
    yonder ash,
Defying wind and rain,
He sung his hymn of courage and of
    faith.

The sun sank to its rest;
The lamps went out;
The last notes died away;
The rain poured down,
And on the hill the storm alone was
    heard.

But more than memory remained to
  me,
The unseen Presence, that is
  ev'rywhere,
Had touched and healed my soul,
The glorious beauty of the raindrops'
  light,
The faith and courage of the
  storncock's song
Were channels of its grace.

Radstock.

CHAPTER THIRTEEN

RADSTOCK II

Before I had been a year in Radstock we had
an Urban District Council election.
Radstock was a small Urban District, of
which there were then several in Somerset.
We were not at that time divided into wards,
but all the candidates ran in one group, and
normally they numbered about forty, and the
top thirteen were declared elected. I was
asked if I would allow myself to be
nominated, and as I am interested in Local
Government, I consented on the

understanding that I stood as an Independent, and that I should not canvass or take any part in the election beyond issuing an address. A few days after I was stopped by a friend, a member of the W.E.A. and of our church council. He began at once, 'I am sorry to see that you have allowed yourself to be nominated for the U.D.C.'

'Why sorry?' I asked, 'I am very interested in Local Government.'

'You have made for yourself,' he said, 'an unusual position in Radstock, you take part in everything, but no party can claim you. If you are elected the Labour Party and the Unionist Party will each try to enlist you, and one of them will succeed, and you will lose the position, which gives you influence with both sides.' I thanked him for his warning, and his last words were 'I shan't vote for you. You are making a mistake'.

In my first election I was second, being eight votes behind the head of the poll. In my second election I was in disgrace with both parties, and this time the manager of the Radstock collieries and myself polled an equal number of votes and tied for the first place. In my last contest I was fairly easily first. It has always been a great pleasure to me that Radstock had sufficient confidence in me to treat me as they did in these elections. Only once in my life has a Bishop offered me preferment, and that was Dr.

Barnes, F.R.S., the Bishop of Birmingham. I am no party man and I love liberty. I believe in liberty whether in ecclesiastical, political or municipal affairs, to be an essential condition of progress. By not a few Conservatives at Radstock I was held to be a Bolshie; by some Labour people, 'a Back Number'. In matters ecclesiastical I have suffered the same fate. The truth is that I am not a party man but a lover of freedom. Happily the fears of my friend proved groundless. Neither party absorbed me. Nor did I ever ask a man or woman for a vote, except through my address.

A clergyman certainly has one natural advantage. In the course of parish work and visiting, one's acquaintance naturally becomes very large, and the people to whom, in one way or another, one has done a good turn, and not few, and that counts, as is illustrated by this incident. I came across a small girl, who was suffering from that painful malady,—a sty in the eye. My youngest boy had lately been rather a persistent victim to the same malady and had been cured by a particular ointment. I fetched some and showed the parents how to apply it. The cure was very speedy. Some months later the election took place. I called on the parents soon after and they told me that Doris whose eye I cured had given them no peace on the polling day until they had both been down to vote for me.

I found the Urban District Council work a most valuable experience. Some of my duties were not pleasant. When I became chairman we decided to inspect personally the closets in all the poorer houses of the place. That night I was sick for four hours. Our sanitary inspector told me that during the course of his duties he had had more than once a similar experience, and that they were not uncommon in his profession.

In March 1924 I stood for the third and last time for election to the Council which was triennial. Some days before the election I had a visit from an old man, who was rather a particular friend of mine. He lived near the church and we often had a chat together. He had been appointed secretary of the Somerset branch of the Miners' Union, when it was first formed, and had long ago retired from that office. He was the bearer of a message, 'The miners are determined that I should be the chairman of the new Council, and if I refused again, they would regard me as having failed in my duty to the parish.' There was only one answer possible, if the chairmanship were offered me, I would accept the office. So in April 1924 I became chairman of Radstock Urban District Council and ex officio a magistrate and I have never regretted it.

As an ex officio J.P. I did not appear on

the Bench unless there was special reason, as I did not wish to risk sitting in judgment on a parishioner, but there were other duties I could not refuse to undertake and one was certifying lunatics. For this purpose it is necessary for the Justice of the Peace to see the patient alone. My first case I was able to certify with assurance. The poor lady received me coldly and speedily told me that she had a commission from God to kill me. I told her that I did not think that could be so, as we had never met before. She affirmed that we had met in Bristol, but I was able to prove an alibi, and she was satisfied that it was a case of mistaken identity. We parted good friends, but I had no difficulty in certifying her to be insane.

At that time I happened upon 'The Fowre Birds of Noah's Arke' by Thomas Dekker (1570–1641) and read his prayer for a magistrate. How strangely different was the magistrate's position then from that of today. 'Thou has called me, O God, being but a worm of the earth, and raised to riches, to riches, as it were, even out of dust, to be a ruler over others; bestow upon me the spirit of wisdom. Humble me, O my Maker, in this top of height; that my head being lifted up to honour, my heart may not swell up with pride.—Grant this and whatsoever else, O Lord, I stand in need of, to guide me in this dangerous sea, wherein Thou has appointed me to sail.'

Ours was an active little Council, very anxious to do its best for the place. Its chief danger, I think, was a practice of political parties to consider matters, which would come before the Council, in private session beforehand and to come to the Council committed to a policy, thus destroying the invaluable process of co-operative thinking with those who may not agree with you.

One excellent piece of work was the erection of a relatively large number of houses built of stone. For this purpose we bought our own quarry, from which we could run the stone on to the site by a tramway. The houses had a good appearance, were well designed, and had good gardens. The rents were exceptionally low, 14/- and 9/- if I remember right, plus some odd pence. I can praise the work, as it was initiated before I had a leading part in policy. Another important piece of work, was completed after I left, was the acquisition of the springs from which we obtained our water supply, and from which we supplied neighbours.

I always found both parties very kind to me, but I put my foot in it one day, not seriously but sadly. We had had a long meeting followed by a committee. As I left the Council office a man came up to ask me about the possibilities of getting a house.

'So,' I said to him, 'We shall have some for allotment shortly.' At our next meeting the chairman of the housing committee brought the matter before the Council—Someone had violated the rule of secrecy, which held with regard to Committees, and suddenly I realised what I had done. I got up at once and apologised, and there was a roar of laughter, and a cry of 'All right, we don't want any more said.' They had had their bit of fun.

We had a very quiet and useful three years and our last meeting coincided with my departure from Radstock.

When I had sat as chairman for the last time, each member got up and said a few nice words of farewell. The thing which pleased me most was the speech of the oldest member, 'I have sat in every Council since Radstock first had one, and this is the first time that the three years of the Council's life has passed without a single row.'

I found not a few of my fellow citizens at Radstock, very attractive and staid men and women, not infrequently referred to wife or husband as 'my sweetheart'. I used to teach regularly in the school twice a week. One day the wife of a miner whom I knew addressed me on my way to school with the words—'You have not seen my sweetheart, have you?' The lady, who addressed me, was the wife of a miner, middle aged, and some would say—'plain', but others would notice the saving grace of her expression.

I could not help her and went on my way, and she resumed her search, but her words had given me a new idea for my lesson.

Prayers were over, and the children had scattered to their classrooms. I was to take the senior boys. The room was separated by a glass partition from the senior girls, and was not impervious to sound. With my brief conversation on the way to school with the lady, who was looking for her husband in mind, I propounded this question to my boys—'Some day you will want to get married. I want to know what sort of woman, you think, would make the right kind of wife, and what ways of doing things, and what kind of qualities you would like her to have? I find it difficult,' I said, 'sometimes to make my meaning clear,' and I told them that I had just been talking to a woman, who was married more than thirty years ago and was still able to call her husband her sweetheart. 'What gifts, graces and quality help to make so great a success of a marriage?' Here I stopped and silence reigned, not only in our classroom but also in that beyond the glass partition. It was one of those silences which are almost solemn. No-one even scratched his head or blew his nose. In the girls' classroom beyond the screen even the teacher was silent and gazing our way.

'Well?' I said, raising my eyebrows, and throwing all the encouragement I could into that small but impressive word.

Then the hush was broken and a clear voice piped out—'a clean woman'. Before me rose the picture of a small room, very tidy, with a tub of hot water steaming before a real collier's fire and a man, still in his 'black skin' just home from the pit, divesting himself of his upper garments. (These were days before there were pit baths.) His wife, with her sleeves rolled up, is preparing to wash his back.

Quickly came the second answer— 'Careful in spending money,' and with it a vision arose of the Co-op crowded with customers on Saturday morning, with housewives planning, and choosing the week's supply of food.

'Well, what next?'—this time there was but little pause—'Not foul mouthed', and from another quarter—'a good housekeeper'.

The game was now well afoot, and one answer followed on another, 'A good neighbour'; 'cheerful'; 'truthful'; 'a good cook'; 'not given to strong drink'; 'can control children'; 'a lover of fair play'. The children know well the value of these virtues.

'Minds her own business'; 'Stand up for her children'. Once more they were picturing the home, a house, one of a row, where a man cannot have words with his wife without all the neighbours knowing, or the children wander from the path outside, without a neighbour's garden suffering. And then the crowning utterance—'Honour her husband'.

A graceless lingering wench who had come with a message put out her tongue. All eyes were turned on her, and the wags were sensing the opportunity, so we passed to the next stage in the lesson.

'Have you met my sweetheart?' This time it was the man who spoke, and she was by his side, and he wanted to introduce her to me. As we shook hands I felt instinctively that she was what the boys had in mind and much besides. Perhaps she had kinship with the heroine of Stevenson's poem,

'Honour, anger, valour, fire:
A love that life could never tire
Death quench or evil stir,
The mighty master
Gave to her.
Teacher tender, comrade, wife,
A fellow farer true through life,
Heart-whole and soul-free,
The August Father
Gave to me.'

While I was at Radstock, I generally went to hear the Speaker at the annual Labour demonstration, which was held out of doors in the summer. In the year before the great stoppage in the coal trade the speaker was Mr. Frank Hodges, then secretary of the Miners' Union. I was accompanied by Captain Stephens, then a churchwarden and head master of the church school. Somehow we found ourselves shortly in the front rank of the crowd around the platform. The first speaker was a little red faced man from Bristol. His eye fell on my collar and his speech digressed and became an exposure of the wickedness and uselessness of the clergy, delivered with such vigour that he fairly dripped with perspiration. The crowd seemed to be getting rather restive, but I listened unabashed. Suddenly I felt a note being thrust into my hand. I glanced down at it. It was brief. 'Leave him to me, Frank Hodges.' The little man ended—red and perspiring, wiping his brow and looking well pleased with himself, but there was very little applause, and Frank Hodges stepped forward. He began by reminding us that we were meeting in Writhlington parish, and that the rector of Writhlington, The Revd. Geoffrey Ramsay, was at the moment sitting as chairman of the Co-operative Congress of Great Britain, which was that very day holding its annual meeting at Bristol. Then he turned on the wretched orator. After his victim had heard a few sentences he could bear no more—but fairly bolted from the scene.

My neighbour, the Revd. G. Ramsey, rector of Writhlington, was a man, who under happier circumstances, should have done first rate work for Christ, the Church and religion, but his lot was unfortunate. He was in many ways a remarkable man. His father had been a most acceptable rector of Writhlington and Foxcote before him, and had done work in the district, the fruit of which was still manifest when I became rector of Radstock nine years after his death. Unfortunately Geoffrey Ramsey succeeded him. He was the man for a great working class parish and should have served under a Bishop like Lightfoot or Westcott—not in the Diocese of Wells, where there was little opening for a man like him, and no appreciation of his quality. He became absorbed in consequence in the Co-operative movement, their directors knew his value. Soon he was asked to become a director of the Radstock Co-operative Society, and a little later of the Co-operative Society of Great Britain. He said to me when he left us—'For eight years I have been rector of a small country parish, and I have done everything I can there. The Co-operative movement has been my only chance of getting adequate work.' Thus a man of real value was lost to the ranks of the parish clergy. It was a grave reflection on the authorities at Wells. The Co-operative

Society knew how to use him, and we heard how he went as their emissary even to Russia at times.

1926 was a dark year. It opened with heavy storm clouds gathering on the horizon of the mining industry. Soon the joy of life seemed clouded over. Then followed the meeting at Newcastle on Tyne of the representatives of the miners, and in a few hours we heard that there was no settlement and industrial war had been declared.

I shall never forget the deep depression into which the news threw me. Our representative at Newcastle was a tried leader of our miners, and a very shrewd and experienced leader he was—a demagogue in the ancient sense, a leader of the people against other parties. He and I used constantly to be in contact through the Council of which I was chairman and the Council School managers, of which I was a member, and he chairman. I heard that he had arrived home and my steps turned to his house. I knew full well that nothing could be done and that obviously my visit was a waste of his time. Yet I wanted to hear from him if there was any ray of hope. He looked desperately tired. He told me how they had sat all the day before and how he had travelled all night to get home quickly. 'No power on earth could change things now.'

The strike notices had gone out and the

men would be out tomorrow.' I think that in his heart of hearts he was pleased by my concern. I did not stay more than a few minutes and his farewell was very cordial.

The strike made no barrier between me and my people to whatever party they belonged.

But what a weary time it was. I was made chairman of the Relief Committee, and did what I could for that. I took an early opportunity to have a talk with our head policeman for as chairman of the Urban District Council since I was an ex officio magistrate and if there were trouble I should be called upon to act. I wanted to know precisely what help he might look for from me, if there were occasion. The Urban District Council was almost equally divided in opinion, but they acted in entire agreement with each other in our new extra duties. In a neighbouring district they had to send a commissioner from London to take charge. I think that our new recreation ground was a great help in keeping the young fellows employed and their minds off their troubles. Football is a good antidote to disorder.

So the days went drearily by. Mr. Cooke, the miners' leader who was born close to Radstock, paid us a visit and held a great open air meeting on the recreation ground. I had a funeral at the church and as I waited for its advent, I could hear his voice rising and falling from across the valley. What a tremendous voice he had!

On the third or fourth week of the strike I had a scare. I had been visiting and as I returned, the Sergeant of Police met me and told me to return at once to the rectory, as a messenger had come through from Taunton with a message for me. Of course, my thoughts flew to special constables, and the prospect of a row. I hurried back and tore open the packet. It contained a copy of the diminutive paper the Government had begun to publish, edited I believe by Winston Churchill—with a request that it might be placed in the public library. With a great sense of relief I took it there.

Meanwhile the conduct of Radstock was admirable. The miners' secretary was a friend of mine, and he gave me great pleasure when we met for the last time years after, as he came out of church when I was revisiting Radstock. We shook hands and he said, 'I often think of those times when you and I were working together during the great strike for the peace of Radstock.'

The weary weeks dragged on and soon families began to suffer, but until quite at the end there was no unhappy incident. Order was admirable. Then there was a great shock. Here and there men had begun under the pressure of home difficulty to try to get back to work. The women are normally the last to desire a strike, but when once out, it is said, they are the most difficult to control. When some men began to go back to work, women stoned them—an unhappy experience for those men, even if women are generally bad shots.

Then a terrible thing happened. One of the mine shafts in the Radstock area is in the middle of the town. At the mouth of the shaft was found by the engineman a case of explosive—enough it was said, to bring all our houses about our ears. The countryside rang with the shame of it, and the London papers reported it and headed it 'An outrage at Radstock'. That night fifty police constables reached Radstock and took up their residence in an empty house on the Wells road. The place was now paraded by police and the ladies of Radstock ceased to throw stones, while men went back to work quietly though at first in small numbers.

There has never been any official explanation of the outrage but all Radstock were quickly satisfied that whatever the explanation of the mystery might be there was no intention to do the town or the collieries any harm. Some said that a man who had been in trouble and who was interested in explosives had put a packet where it would do most damage, and there he himself found it, and reported it, and as he seemed to have saved the mine, his fault was forgiven. Another explanation was that someone deeply interested in the return of the men to work, arranged for the explosive to be put where it was found.

I met the police officer in charge, an old friend of mine, or he was in earlier days at Radstock, and we walked down Wells Hill together. 'Well! Have you got your man,' I asked—'No,' he replied, 'but I could lay my hand on him in an hour if I wanted to,' and his eyes twinkled. But everyone was happy now, for the strike had come to an end, so why ask questions about explosives? No one was the worse for them, or ever meant to be, and the strike had come to an end which was the thing that mattered.

In the porch of Radstock church hung the photographs of some rectors of Radstock.

The earliest of the photographs is a miniature of the Rev. Richard Boodle, who became rector in 1814 and held the office until his death nearly forty years later. He was already an old man when the miniature was painted, and was seated in a chair, holding in his hands a stick with a carved ivory top. His frock coat is buttoned tightly around him and his chin, pressed down upon his white stock, is flanked by an ample collar. The face crowned with white hair is long and thoughtful with a nose markedly aquiline. His disposition was gentle and placid. He was one of those rare people who can take up a handful of bees without rousing their resentment. He used to enjoy a gallop on Clandown of his mare, Blackberry, and could repaint his carriage himself when it began to look shabby, but he had more significant interests than these.

During his incumbency Radstock changed from a country parish to a characteristically colliery parish. The batches crept slowly out from the hillsides. The trees disappeared. Rows of miners' cottages were built, where the ground was level enough for their foundations. The streams lost their brightness and their trout. The aspect of Radstock's valleys became grim and untidy. It is significant that like Skinner, his neighbour at Camerton, Mr. Boodle built a little school—within a few yards of the beautiful church porch. I think that he saw dimly what in days to come it might mean to the lives of his parishioners. It would help to awaken their souls, and in it he himself often used to teach.

His great interest was the health of his parishioners. There is a tradition that he was educated to be a doctor. At any rate he and his wife used to dispense medicines at the rectory and the parish registers in his day betray more than an amateur interest in public health.

In the register of burials there is damning

evidence of what child labour below ground might mean, as the following entries illustrate.

Frederick Bond, Aug. 20 1820 age 12. Head fractured by the kick of a horse C/D (Clandown) Coal pit.

George Chappel, Nov. 26. 1824. age 8 years, killed by falling down L (Ludless) coal pit. (Men were in those days lowered into the pit clinging to a rope with a leg through a loop. Little boys would normally sit astride a man's knee.)

Joseph Parfitt, Nov. 16. 1842 aged 9 years. Killed by bad air in a coal pit.

James Withers, April 11. 1847, aged 11 years. Killed in W.W. (Wells Way Pit) by a stone falling on him.

Until the middle of the nineteenth century small boys were numbered among the victims of the colliery. Joseph Parfitt must have been among the last killed under the age of ten.

What the rector thought about it, is not expressed in any words that have survived. Probably he felt helpless to mend the matter and at any rate Parliament was beginning to be interested. These facts are recorded in the church register.

In regard to hours the evidence of the Royal Commission found that 'In some coal mines in this district the regular hours of work are only from 8 to 10 in number, but more often they are from 10 to 12 and occasionally they are prolonged to 13.' The only holidays were Christmas Day, Good Friday and a day or two at Whitsuntide for the Friendly Society celebrations, but there were periods in which work was short at the colliery through lack of orders or a breakdown of the machinery, and then it was 'No work, no wages' and something approaching starvation.

Where the rector could help he did. The parish was periodically swept by epidemics— among other by typhus, small pox and cholera. One person died from the bite of a mad dog; in one six months three children died for burns. In regard to small pox at least, the rector could do something, for Jenner's life's work was completed about the time that he became rector of Radstock. On small pox the rector waged active war. In the year 1838 small pox was very generally prevalent throughout England and more than usually fatal. In the parish seven people died of this dreadful disease. Four of these had refused vaccination. 'Of the others Benjamin Chivers aged nine months had been vaccinated but the vaccination did not take effect. The mother put the child into bed with a child who had the small pox full upon him. He caught the small pox and had it very severely and pustules formed on the balls of both eyes and the eyes perished and the child died a month or two afterwards.'

'George Cottle aged one year and three months had been vaccinated by me in his infancy, but it had failed, and I told his parents that it must be done again, when an opportunity offered, but it was not done.' 'Emma Gulliford, aged nine. She was the only one of the family whom I had not vaccinated, but this was through a mistake not negligence of the parents. She was born just at the time when I had been vaccinating the rest of the family and parish and neighbourhood. I then did not vaccinate again for three years. Then the parents brought a young child for vaccination, but omitted to bring Emma, supposing she had been vaccinated with her elder brothers and sisters.'

Thus the old rector strove to banish small pox from his parish but it must often have been with vexation of spirit. We can almost hear as we read these entries the reproaches of Mr. and Mrs. Cottle and the protest of the rector—'But I told you that it must be done again,' and the vain regret of the parents and parson alike for poor little George.

The victory was in time won. Small pox has been practically banished. Yet, when I was rector, not one third probably of those who lived in Radstock, had been vaccinated or had any intention of submitting to it; and in my last years I was constantly approached by people who sought exemption from vaccination for their children.

The second photograph is that of the Rev. Nelson Ward who was rector in 1853. He was the grandson of Lord Nelson and of Lady Hamilton. He was still remembered by many when I came to the parish—a very tall man with a very short wife, who were often seen walking together arm in arm—a couple held in high regard by the parishioners, and deeply attached to each other.

The church at Radstock in earlier days if the witness of its ancient porch speaks true, must have been a thing of beauty, for that has a stone barrel roof carved with quatrefoils and bosses of animals and faces.

The church was enlarged about 1830 and the service of Thanksgiving which was attended by the Rev. John Skinner, rector of the neighbouring parish of Camerton, was held on August 2nd 1832. The sermon was preached by the Rec. Trelawny Collins, who rather strangely chose as his text the utterance of Jacob, when he awoke from sleep at Bethel. 'How dreadful is this place!' His selection of that text gave great joy to the Rev. John Skinner, vicar of Camerton, and author of a journal and an antiquarian, who knew not a little of architecture. One of the misdeeds of the architect was to turn the ancient Norman font out of the church. Years after it was discovered being used as a drinking trough for cattle in a neighbouring farmyard by one who in later days was my churchwarden, Mr. Howard Coombs. He caused it to be restored to its proper place. I wonder how much there was of beauty and interest was destroyed at that time. Soon after I came to Radstock an idea struck me. The head of the ancient parish cross had been set in a window in the porch. It was a fine piece of stonework, presenting on one side the Virgin and the Babe and on the other the Crucifixion. Where was the rest of the Cross?

As I walked past the chancel of the church I had often wondered what the history of a fragment of a stone shaft was, which protruded some two feet from the turf beside the path. The sexton used to sit on it when waiting for a funeral. Could this be a bit of the shaft of the ancient Church Cross? At our next meeting of the Church Council, I asked for any information they could give about it, but none was forthcoming, and then I told them my surmise. They were mostly miners and here was something in their line. 'We'll dig it up and see what it is.' So we agreed to explore the mystery on the next Saturday afternoon at 3 p.m. At the appointed hour there was quite a crowd assembled, and as it struck three, I gave the word and two or three stepped forward, armed with pick and shovel. In a few minutes the great cube of stone, which formed the calvary of the old Cross, lay on the turf with about 3 feet of the shaft intact. They explored further, but found nothing more of note.

After consultation with Mr. Eeles, then secretary of 'the Society for the Preservation of Ancient Churches', we decided to place this treasure in the church against the west wall and to take the head of the Cross from its exposed place in the window and to attach it to the top of the remains of the shaft. He personally superintended what we did. This was the first of three discoveries.

The next I owed to Dr. Coulton of Cambridge, a specialist on medieval history. We were standing in the vestry talking when he suddenly said—'Hullo, do you know what that is?' indicating a scratching of a minstrel girl on the wall close to the entrance to the tower stairway. I had often noticed it and surmised that it was the work of some idle fellow, who had thus occupied himself while waiting, perhaps, for the rest of the ringers. 'That is fifteenth century work,' he said.

'How do you know that?' I asked.

'By the dress of course,' he replied.

I caused a frame to be put around it, and glass over it, with a few words on it, indicating the interest of what it had enclosed.

The meaning of a third discovery has only

recently come to light. For more than twenty years now a great stone had lain in the porch, which bears the letters printed in the margin of this page

```
Z
D E
N E C O R
O N I
M O T
V I X
V ? R
V E N
F V Q
Q V O
```

It came out of a grave in the churchyard not far from the south wall. The sexton was actually fetching a hammer to break it up, when happily, Captain Stephens, then churchwarden, passed and asked him why he wanted that tool. He had noticed the lettering and had the stone removed to the church porch. I failed to get any interpretation of it at the time though I made various efforts.

Quite lately I was in communication with the curator of the Roman baths and museum at Bath and Mr. Anthony, the curator, has most kindly given me the following description and explanation of the stone and inscription.

Report on the Inscribed Stone in

'The stone measures 3ft 6ins from the base to the highest point on the top, which has been badly damaged, and weathered. It is 11 inches wide: the left hand having a three inch margin separated from the inscribed portion by a vertical line. The right hand of the stone bears tool marks, which show that it was cut, possibly in the Roman period, but more probably since then in order that the stone be reused for building purposes. The depth of 9½–10 inches and as the fragment appears to be about a third of the original, it must have formed a very substantial monument ... Most of the inscription is doubtful as so much is missing, but it seems probable that it is a tombstone set up by the heirs of an infantry soldier, who served in an auxiliary cohort and later in a Legionary unit. Further investigation into this type of memorial may reveal more information.

J. E. Anthony
Curator of the Roman Baths & Museum, Bath.
Oct. 13. 1952.'

We did a great deal of work for the improvement of Radstock church, much of which is recorded in Mr. Arthur Mee's Guide to Somerset. We were fortunate in having the help of my eldest daughter,

Clemency who was an expert carver. Her main work was the carving of the war memorial screen in front of the vestry in the East End on which are recorded the names of those who died in the two great wars. She also painted the ceiling of the tower vestry and carved a Tudor Rose for the centre of it. But the most original work and that which attracted Mr. Arthur Mee's special attention, was the list of the rectors. It seemed dull to record merely names and dates so my daughter and I designed one illustrated by small painting on gold leaf. We had no difficulty in selecting subjects and each name has its illustration. Here are some of our explanations.

In 1400 the new tower appears, and circa 1425 the Churchyard Cross. In 1462 Parson Biggs is represented as flying in his surplice from the altar before a wrathful Yorkist lady with the inscription—'An overmighty subject drove Parson Biggs away'. In 1549 the incumbent, seated in the Church with a book in his hand, is asking—'What do you think of our new Prayer Book?' Another represents one of Judge Jeffrey's acorns hanging from a great oak, which used to stand on Well's Way road. In 1819 the miners are represented facing the 17th Lancers on Clandown, with their cry, 'Bread or Blood', painted on below. In 1825 William Ashman is trying his locomotive engine, which just failed to be a success, and next is Parson Boodle vaccinating his parishioners. These represent some of our subjects. I have never heard of a similar illustrated Clergy Record, and I am rather surprised that no other parish has adopted the idea. Mr. Mee says in his book on Somerset—'What we remember of Radstock is something we rarely remember of any church—the Rector's list. It was done at the rectory, when Canon Bax was there with his artist daughter, and we can almost see them enjoying the work of making up this bit of village history. We have seen no other Rector's list like it, and we found it more interesting than a hundred of last year's novels.'

My daughter also designed and carved some bench ends at Penselwood. Mr. Arthur Mee had not realised that this was also her work.

The principal subjects were the ancient village trades, especially those of the farmer and forester, for Penselwood is, in what was in old days, Selwood Forest.

Both there and at Radstock she included a list of some parishioners of many generations ago on a panel. That at Penselwood, taken from an Exchequer roll of 1315, includes the name 'Butt' probably an ancestor of Mr. Wilfred Butt, who cut and prepared the locally grown oak wood for her.

That at Radstock recorded the names of the Ablemen of the Tithing of Radstock in 1569.

William Simms	Archer
Thos. Gane	Billman
Roger Cottle	Billman
Thos. Tucker	Pikeman
John Atkyns	Archer
John Bretton	Archer
John Teuke	Billman

I think that all the names except 'Teuke' survived in the parish when I was rector.

Just before I left, my daughter painted a large sundial on the South Wall of the Church. Under it is the verse which appears on a clock in Chester Cathedral.

When as a child I laughed and wept,
  Time crept.
When as a youth I waxed more bold,
  Time strolled.
When I became a full grown man,
  Time ran.
When older still I daily grew,
  Time flew.
Soon I shall find passing on,
  Time gone.

Written by Canon Henry Twells, 1823–1900 who was an Honorary Cannon of

Peterborough, rector of Waltham-on-the-Wolds Leics. and author of the hymn 'At even, ere the sun was set'. About the time that the Strike began, or 'the stoppage in the coal trade' as it was more tactfully described, we made a new venture at the church. The old fourteenth century tower was reported to be in need of repair and was inspected by Mr. Caroê, the architect of the Ecclesiastical Commissioners. That the tower had been struck by lightning at some time, he pointed out to me as we were looking at it. Very soon we had his report, and the tenders for the work, when they came, were distressing. There was none for a less sum than about £400. That does not seem much today, but the value of money was different in those days, and virtually all our people were on strike. The Church Council looked depressed. They no doubt remembered that there is not much to show for money spent on repairs. To pay for building a tower would scarcely be a harder task than to raise that money for what makes no show.

To break the silence, I threw out a suggestion. 'Can we repair the tower ourselves?' Here was a practical proposition and we began to discuss it.

Four of us volunteered to try. There was Tom Griffen, the engine driver. He was a first rate person. There was Bill Watts, whose job it was to repair the colliery shafts

286

and often to hang by a rope when he worked, if the trouble was in the shaft itself. He was a man with the most valuable experience. There was Taylor, a boot hand, who sung in the choir. There was a man who was strong but who needed careful direction and myself. To our team we added Martin, a skilled mason whom we paid—slightly. He was not a member of the church but a friend. I saw that we were all properly insured. We began with the roof of the tower, which required new beams. The waggon works made us a present of them, but it was a hard task getting the old ones out—their ends had suffered badly from beetle. They were above the bells, and the footholds were none too good. Then we had to get the new beams up. I shall never forget standing on the tower floor, steadying them as they began their upward journey and seeing above me the face of one of our workers who was preparing to guide them in their passage through the trap door. From the floor below the bells, to their places under the lead roof we had to manhandle the new beams. The first took an hour and a quarter to get into position, but the others followed quickly.

Then there was a tile stitch to make in the side of the tower—ten feet by two and carried out to the outermost stone. Not even our mason knew what a tile stitch was, so I had to get directions from Mr. Caroê. I did not tell him that we were doing the work ourselves and he was much surprised that the people, who were doing the work, did not know. 'You take away the wall to the outermost stone and then float in tiles in cement, making them overlap to half their length.' That is substantially the directions he gave us. It was his own invention he told us. At any rate it was a capital invention and we carried out instructions meticulously. When the cement had gone hard, the cracked piece of wall had been replaced by a mass of tiles and cement one in itself and one also with the rest of the wall. But I was very glad when we were able to begin that process of filling in.

We had carefully shored up the beams above the stitch but I was still more glad when we had finished that part of the job.

We followed the architect's directions most carefully throughout and his final letter after he had learnt who did the work, and he had inspected it, was very pleasant reading for us:—

'I feel that I ought to write to you after my visit to Radstock yesterday and tell you how pleased I am with the work done by your voluntary workers, which undoubtedly does them great credit. I feel especially congratulatory upon the masterly way in which they have introduced the stitch across the crack in the north wall. It may interest you to know that I invented this method of stitching myself some 35 years ago, and it has now come into general use among those who understand old buildings, although of course it is equally serviceable when used across defects in modern buildings. I was very pleased with the way in which they had woven the ends of the stitch into the irregularities of the stone work, that being one of the important considerations in the success of the work.

'Perhaps one of your excellent volunteer workers may be able to invent a less perilous access to the leads. I was reminded of "The Cavalier's notebook"—a record of a Roman Catholic reclusant of the times of the Puritan persecutions: "he was evidently a man of parts in more ways than one and described one of his hiding holes as 'a straight for a fat man'".' I hope you will be able to carry through the new bell frame in due course. I can generally save most old ones, but yours is past saving I'm afraid.

'You might pass on one of my precepts which I commend to the notice of your workers—Never use cement against the atmosphere; excellent as it is inside a well when covered up on the surface.

Yours sincerely,
W. D. Caroê'

The bell frames were replaced after I left, and the ringers lowered them themselves from their places in the tower and sent me a photograph of them set out on the turf. The same spirit, as was in our team, was still there.

We also received a latter of congratulation from the Archdeacon on behalf of the advisory committee of the diocese.

20. Dec. 27.
St Michael's Glastonbury

My dear Bax, I received Caroê's comment on the work which you have done on the tower at Radstock to the advisory committee and I am to send you our hearty congratulations on the pluck and skill of all who took part in it.

Yours very sincerely,
Walter Farrer.

My team appreciated very much this letter, but no word came from the Palace, which was, I think, a pity.

CHAPTER FOURTEEN

RADSTOCK III

One sad tragedy happened in our garden. Dear Brown Willy Owlie who had accompanied us from Duloe to Long Benton, from Long Benton to Maperton, from Maperton to Radstock, took up his residence in a small garden house at the bottom of the lawn, and there he lived virtually free. My last recollection of him is sitting on a branch of a tree near the house and being fed with mice sent by a neighbouring farmer for Owlie when they killed a great number while threshing a rick. Owlie ate so many that the tail of the last for which he had no room, hung out of his beak. That is the last vision I have of Owlie alive. I do not know if owls ever suffer from indigestion. Perhaps the crop is devised by nature to save them from it. One morning, shortly later, I splashed down in my gumboots to open his door, and let him fly out. Poor dear Owlie! When I opened the door I saw his body floating on the water, dead, for the flood had penetrated the house. He must have fallen off his perch for he should have been quite safe. I could have cried when I saw him. He was an old friend from Duloe days, and with him were bound up so many recollections and associations.

I noticed one of our policemen examining the doors of our drive very carefully. 'What were you looking for?' I asked him, 'I was looking for beggars' marks,' he said. Beggars sometimes recorded their impression of the people who lived in a house, for the guidance of their kind.

'What do they say on our gates?' I asked. 'I can't find any today,' he answered. 'There was one the other day, but I removed it.' 'Was it very bad?' I asked. 'Not too bad,' he replied. 'It was not bad on the whole.'

Our modern legislation had relieved the clergy of one of the most difficult of our dealings with the class of callers, common in old days, but now never seen. To determine what to do about beggars, was a very unpleasant part of our duties. Modern legislation has cleared our roads of them. In old days beggars were numerous and many of them lazy and dishonest scoundrels. On the other hand the lack of provision to the man or woman genuinely out of work made it impossible just to send them away wholesale. We might be sending away someone genuinely in trouble. The disappearance of the beggar is one of the blessings of my later life as a clergyman. Some of course were people who rightly sought help and we were only too glad to help so far as we could. Here is an example.

I always remember the visit of a man, his wife, and three little girls. They were on their way from Watchett, I think to London. The man was in the motor trade and had gone there to a garage for the summer season in the hope that he might get work as an extra hand, but the summer was wet and there were no visitors and he was discharged. Now he was on his way back to London. The distance from Radstock was well over 100 miles, his money was just finished; a wheel had come off the perambulator. He and his wife were worn out and the children crying. Where could they sleep?

I called my wife and we consulted for a moment or two. The mother said she was an ex hospital nurse and her appearance, and that of the children, looked as if that might be so and they were decent people in trouble. My wife knew the hospital she mentioned, and a question or two showed that the mother did too.

'We can't take you in.' I said, 'It's holiday time and we are full up, but if it will suit you, we will put a big mattress in the bicycle house where you can all sleep comfortably, and we will give you supper and breakfast.'

We showed them the bicycle house and they jumped at it. I went off to arrange for the mending of the perambulator, my wife to collect a good meal, they to have a wash.

They had a good square meal and settled in the bicycle house. I had to rouse them up for breakfast at 9 a.m. when there was still no sign of movement. When we said goodbye, each little girl in turn without any prompting, walked up to me, put her arms around my neck, and bestowed on me a kiss. I have never forgotten those kisses. They are a very pleasant recollection.

All beggars were offered a good meal which was eaten in the boot cleaning shed on special china kept for such occasions. If I felt a beggar was genuine in trying to get home I lodged his fare with the station master who was instructed only to hand over a ticket. This offer was often not taken up—it was a visit to a pub he hoped for!

An urgent need of the parish of Radstock was youthwork. There was in existence a useful branch of the Girls' Friendly Society, but little for boys. Under the inspiring leadership of our choirmaster, Captain Stephens, churchwarden and schoolmaster the choir became really strong, and we used to have the boys at the rectory on Monday evenings for games, so that we got to know them well. We often had a joke with them of one kind or another. One evening, as it was growing dark, I slipped away and in the shrubbery took my elder daughter on my shoulders, arrayed in a top hat and a long Inverness cape and we thus appeared, as a gigantic figure. I moved slowly in the dimness across the lawn towards the dining room with its French windows where the boys were playing. I heard one call out—'Gosh, there's a giant coming across the lawn!' and dead silence fell on the room as they gazed out of the window, and then rushed suddenly from the room to the kitchen, to the young maids who were Radstock girls. We went to the front door and knocked loudly. There was a delay and whispering and then the door was opened cautiously by the maids—the boys peeping from behind them.

Jokes like these are trifles, but we had many bits of fun together. Years later, I happened to travel in the same carriage as two of the mothers of these choir boys. We recognised each other, and they told us how old choir boys still, when they met together, used to recall the Sunday evening fun at the rectory.

Our organist was blinded by a bow and arrow as a child. He was brought up at the Blind Institution at Birmingham where he met his future wife who went blind after a serious illness. She bore him eleven children, none of whom of course had any defect of sight, and the eldest of whom became a signalman in the Navy; the second was in the 17th Lancers. Mr. Parker in course of his business as a teacher of music used to walk anywhere within four miles of Radstock for that purpose. Only once was he lost. He was returning home to Radstock after giving a lesson on a dark night when three or four inches of snow lay on the ground and he had to cross Clandown. He always depended on his feet to tell him if he were on the road. Four inches of snow caused them to fail him. He could not feel the road, and he wandered on to the down, where he was found in the early morning. He had a wonderful instinct for knowing where he was. For pure curiosity people who gave him a lift, used to stop suddenly, and ask him to say where they were, and report said that he was always right.

Some of our choir trips together are unforgettable. They coupled a long day and the choir would take their music and if possible sing in this or that beautiful church. I shall never forget one in which our ultimate objective was Porlock Weir on the other side of the county. It was a lovely day followed by a lovely evening and nightfall. At Dunster we trooped into the beautiful old Priory Church. The choir were practising, and in a few minutes their choir and our choir were singing alternately their favourite anthems. It was difficult to tear ourselves away. We did not reach home until after midnight and the younger boys were lying in all sort of postures on the floor and seats of the charabanc plunged in profound sleep.

Our Church of England Men's Society and Mothers' Union run by my wife together with the choir and ringers formed a practice which might well become common. We used to arrange with certain neighbouring parishes, who were on unusually friendly terms with ourselves, a parish visit on a summer evening. It would begin with a pull at the bells, then a short service in church, at which some layman of our or their church gave a brief address. This was followed by an entertainment, for which one of the parishes was responsible for songs etc, and of course there were refreshments. These visits were most enjoyable, and also wholesome from parish and rurideacanal points of view.

We did much for the school while I was in Radstock. We greatly improved the Head Master's house. We bought rather more than an acre of land next to the churchyard, got the friendly Council of Radstock to tip on it and then put back the soil and made a small field of just over an acre, sufficient for boys' football and cricket. We turned the stream and made a good hard piece of ground for the infants to play on, and with an old tree, under which they could sit in the summer and have lessons out of doors. We also took advantage of an opportunity and bought a nice garden for a school garden and to make possible instruction in poultry keeping. I put in a good many hours of hard work myself into making the small field possible for football and cricket, and was rather pleased when a miner friend passing one day said to me, 'We shall never want a monument of you here, rector. We shall always think of you working on this ground.'

The Council School of which I was a manager followed suit and also secured a small field for cricket and football. These little fields were a great gain to the schools.

Alas! for what followed! When I last saw it the War Office had built a small strong point on the infants' playground which had not been removed. The small field which we had reclaimed and tipped was spoilt by the erection of a place for school dinners, so cricket and football were no longer possible. They might just as well have gone across the road, and bought a patch from the glebe field. It was now 1928 and nearly eleven years had passed since I had been instituted to Radstock. They had been happy years, but the work had been hard, and I had had no holiday in all that time, except an occasional few days between Sundays, and my short holiday abroad after an operation. The holiday I needed most was a change of work, but of that I saw no prospect whatever. Then, as it were in a moment, all was changed. In a clergyman's life changes, when they come, are often sudden and unexpected. So it was with me.

A knock on the door awakened me. I turned over wearily and looked for my teacup on the tray. There was a letter there as well, but I drank my tea before I picked that up. What I needed was a change of work. I put down my cup and picked up the letter. It bore the Birmingham postmark, I noticed, but that caused no thrill and suggested nothing. I knew no one there. I had visited it not long before, as a diocesan representative at a great Copec meeting in company with the Revd. Noel Waldegrave, who afterwards succeeded his brother in the Waldegrave peerage. I opened the letter but suddenly raised myself to sitting posture and read carefully. It was from the Bishop of Birmingham, and was an invitation to come and see him with a view to becoming vicar of Moseley in succession to the Venble. C. E. Hopton, Archdeacon of Birmingham, who was resigning the living, which he had held hitherto as well as the Archdeaconry.

My wife and I went to Birmingham, and stayed a night with the Bishop and Mrs. Barnes, and saw the churchwardens, and the church and vicarage. A little later we visited Birmingham again and met the Church Council, whom we found very friendly, and the appointment was made. It was a great wrench leaving Radstock. I had been very happy there and was much attached to its people. I cannot visit it even now after the lapse of years without my heart warming to the place, and its inhabitants. Yet it was time for me to leave. A change of parish now and again, with the new experience it brings, is, I think, normally necessary to the full development of a clergyman's powers, especially if the work in them is somewhat of a different nature. The change itself also is in a sense a rest. At Moseley too, I expected to have a curate and in consequence the possibility of getting away for much needed holidays. The type of work was different. Moseley was residential, and its people worked in the great city, of which it was a suburb.

CHAPTER FIFTEEN

MOSELEY

On the day of the announcement of my appointment to Moseley, I went to Bath on business, and chanced to meet there a diocesan magnate. We shook hands and exchanged opinions on the weather, which we did not praise, but he had a more important subject on his mind, and after a brief labour it was brought to birth. 'I hear that you are appointed to Moseley. Do you think that you will ever get on there?' He paused and looked at me severely—in a way that suggested that the correct and natural answer was an emphatic 'No!' 'Time will show,' I replied, 'but of one thing you may rest assured—I shall do my best.' We parted, and no doubt he felt that if, after this warning, I went to Moseley and failed, I should have no one to blame but myself. The change itself was in a sense a rest, and there was this gain. Most of us make mistakes. We leave these behind us, and as perhaps a wiser, and it should be a better, man we make a new start. The type of parish to which I was going was very different from Radstock. Radstock was typically a mining district and the centre of the Somerset coalfield. Birmingham is the second largest city of the Empire, and Moseley is a very important suburb of that city.

The vicarage was the size of a small country house. The hall was big enough for a dance of fifteen or twenty couples, and was thus used on occasion by our children and their friends. It was also of great use for parish purposes. In it we held on one occasion a successful sale of pictures for a lady artist, who suffered from a loss of market in the war. On another we had a sale of unwanted goods for a lady who had fallen on hard times, and thus raised an amount towards the purchase of a small annuity for her. I saw it at fullest when the then Bishop of Lichfield addressed a gathering of over 80 businessmen. On that occasion they were sitting on the stairs as well as in the hall. We had, in the summer, a market for the S.P.G. in our garden, and the hall was then of the greatest value. In the dining room beyond the hall for three or four years running, we had an exhibition illustrating great men and women of Moseley. We used to ask for a photograph if they were still alive. I have a very nice autographed copy of H. V. Morton's 'In the Steps of the Master', which was bought in at a good price and handed to me by the purchaser. Mr. Morton in days gone by had lived in Moseley. Then there was Highbury in the parish—the original home of the Chamberlains—which, after they left, became successively a hospital for wounded soldiers, and then a Home for aged women.

Happily, not only for us, but for a good many others as well, the extensive cellarage, strongly reinforced and its second exit improved, became a popular shelter in the bad days to come—although owing to numbers at times, the refugees had to be content with the hall, or even the study, to sleep in.

It is worthwhile to recall the earlier history of Moseley. Originally it was part of the enormous parish of Bromsgrove, now a small town some twelve miles away. Kings Norton was first parted from Bromsgrove, and we became part of the new parish. Then in the opening of the fifteenth century the first church at Moseley was built by the parishioners of Kings Norton because that parish was seven miles broad everyway and forty miles compass and many of the parishioners lived seven miles from their parish church. In 1405 a licence was given to the parishioners of Kings Norton to attend Mass in the parish of St. Mary's, Moseley. Of the original church only the tower remains, and that has quite recently and deservedly been declared a national monument.

In succession a second church in 1514 took the place of the original building, and a third in turn in 1780. The fourth church was an attempt by Thomas Rickman, a pioneer of the Gothic revival, to convert a Georgian building into a Gothic one.

Two of our former vicars have been men of more than local mark.

The Rev. William, vicar 1684–6, was a moral philosopher. Of his book *The Religion of Nature Delineated*, over ten thousand copies are said to have been sold—an enormous number in those days. A copy of it, which I secured, lies in a glass case in the church. He wrote mostly in his own shorthand. His book attracted the notice of the very able consort of George III, Queen Caroline, and she placed his bust in her garden house, where she collected the busts of notable men of her day.

The second was Walter Farquhar Hook, D.D., F.R.S., perpetual curate of Moseley 1826–28. He was afterwards vicar of Leeds and Dean of Chichester. There is a story which records how he tramped the parish to raise funds to found a school.

When I came to Moseley I had no idea that it had been the boyhood home of my dear old Bishop, Brook Foss Westcott, and only realised that when I discovered the grave of his father and mother in our churchyard.

I have already spoken of the interest which the improvement of the church and churchyard became to the congregation at Radstock, and of the reaction of this common interest on our church life. Moseley parish church offered another wonderful opportunity. My predecessors, the Rev. Canon Colmore and more especially Archdeacon Hopton, had done a great work for the fabric, but much remained to be done.

The story of Moseley parish is characteristic of the growth of Birmingham.

Clerestory and the south aisle took the place of the Rickman Church 1910 and choir vestry and sacristy were in due course added.

All this work was done during the incumbencies of Canon Colmore and Archdeacon Hopton. It was my good fortune to become vicar at this stage, and at a time when the dormant artistic sense of Birmingham was fast awakening and increasing. We also had an excellent architect in Mr. Philip Chatwin, F.R.I.B.A. F.S.A., to advise and guide. When I came to Moseley the shell of the building was complete. It remained to adorn it.

We began modestly with the side chapel, a building which can seat nearly a hundred people. A screen at the main entrance took the place of a curtain. It was refloored and a new window was pierced, which gave it light. Eighteenth century panelling from St. Bartholomew's, Birmingham, which was closed in 1938, was re-erected at Moseley: such changes carried out through a church made a great difference to its appearance. For instance, we, with the consent of the donor, removed a brass tablet recording the name of the person commemorated by a screen between the chancel and the side chapel, and had the inscription carved on the screen itself, which was an enrichment of the memorial.

All the church, except the chancel and the north aisle, had been built of the beautiful mottled Hollington stone from Staffordshire.

I should like to recall how what was

perhaps the most important piece of the work in my time was begun. In Oxford Road there lived at that time a Mr. Halsey, who used to come to the church very regularly on Sunday mornings, and sit in the south aisle. We both had country tastes, and from time to time I used to look in on him. One summer evening the talk turned on the church, and I deplored the appearance of the north wall and north door. He said, 'Let us go across and look at it.' He looked at the north door from within and without. 'Yes,' he said, 'this door won't do. The door of a Church should be wide and welcoming, and the steps leading up to it should be the same.' Then he made his offer. 'Look here, I will pay for remaking of the door and steps, and for the relining of the porch wall at that angle of the church with mottled Hollington Stone, so that it may match the beautiful stonework in the south aisle of the church. Perhaps others will take up the idea.' They did, and you can read the inscription of their names cut in the stone, and Mr. Stevens finished that part of the work by the great gift of paying for the relining of the chancel. Thus that dreary north wall became a thing of the past.

The work which was an act of faith was immediately set in hand, the place of the unworthy door was taken by what he used to describe as a 'welcoming doorway' which seemed to invite people in, and which was filled with beautiful oak doors. When Mr. Halsey stood and contemplated the work, he said, 'I never dreamed that I should spend some hundred pounds on work in a church.' But he did not repent of what he did, but immediately arranged that the doors should be approached by a path from the back entrance properly paved, as a suitable approach to the 'welcoming door'. At the time of his death he had in mind the improvement of the entrance to the churchyard on the north side.

This example fired other members of the congregation. In quick succession the other four bays and the spandals of the arches were taken in hand as memorials and the cost of the west end of the north aisle was defrayed by a collection on our Dedication Festival. The whole was a fine illustration of the effect of a bold example. The work was crowned by the refacing of the chancel, in memory of his wife, by my churchwarden, Mr. Robert Stevens, to whom I owe so much.

It would be wearisome to detail the many improvements that were made by the help of a generous and thoroughly interested congregation, but the following note may serve as a suggestion to others. We had in the church some good early nineteenth century mural tablets. Six of these were by William or Peter Hollins, both of whom have won the honour of being included in the Dictionary of National Biography. We set our faces utterly against brasses, and encouraged people to have memorial inscriptions carved on the stone if they could not be carved on the gift itself. The lettering was designed by our architect and executed by a man who was a real artist. They were, I think, a great success. In this way, too, we got rid of some unsightly tablets.

Another pleasure was to revive in the church the memory of notable men who have been connected with it. Moseley was a very insignificant place until quite near the end of the century.

There is one Church Council Meeting in particular which lives in my memory. A proposal was put forward to do away with the pews in the north aisle, and to substitute chairs. The refacing of the wall was such a beautiful addition to the chancel that I was greatly attracted by the proposal. The question was debated for two hours by the Committee, and was lost by a small majority. I feel now that, much as I deplored the covering of so much beautiful stone work, on the whole the majority were right in their decision. But I mention this not to revive past controversy, but because the two hours debate lives in my memory as one in which no provocative word was said. Sides were sharply divided. There was no possibility of compromise. But the debate and its issue accepted by all as the end, without any lasting division, was a model of how a Council should debate questions. I hope and believe that it is still the spirit of Moseley Church Council. I was very fortunate in my Church Council, which was outstanding in its business capacity and helpfulness, and the atmosphere of its meetings was that of a body of friends. I owe very much to their ability and helpfulness, and our meetings were delightfully friendly. For a time all was well at Moseley, and the days passed happily. We took our full part in a great church extension movement. I became chairman of the Sites and Boundaries Committee, the General Committee and the Executive Committee. We had an excellent secretary in Canon Lucas, and outstanding lay helpers in Mr. Deykin and Mr. Bryson, who had given the diocese of Birmingham such notable voluntary help in the diocesan office. We spent many afternoons in the interesting task of exploring Birmingham and framing proposals for new parishes where the population had spread and increased into the country districts around Birmingham. The City Corporation were splendidly helpful. We used to spend long afternoons going from place to place in a conveyance provided by the Corporation, viewing the new districts and choosing the right sites for churches, and sketching their boundaries.

Another side of the work was the raising of the hundred thousand guineas required, which was successfully achieved with a fair surplus above our mark. I was now Rural Dean of Kings Norton, which was on the growing side of Birmingham with an enormous population in some 30 parishes. I arranged a Gift Day Service for the Bishop's Appeal for one hundred thousand guineas. The result was a triumphant success. Our Gift Day was the first of a series of thirteen arranged for the diocese. I am a great believer in action in a service where obviously and naturally it can bring out the meaning and intention of a service. The Bishop began his address by saying 'This service is probably unique in the history of the diocese.' He had striven to make it so. Fifteen of the parishes in the Deanery took part in it. The large church was full, and in the seats along the wall in the north and south aisles sat more than two hundred people, who came to represent their parishes and their organisations in the procession of offering. The service began with prayer for the renewal of life in the church in Birmingham and throughout the world.

Grant to us, O Lord, the listening ear that we may hear what the Spirit saith unto the Churches.

310

Preserve us, O Lord, from the besetting snare of men, to think that we may live by bread alone.

Show us, O Lord, the path of discipleship and teach us how to walk therein.

Give us, O Lord, the willing heart that we may arise and do Thy Will.

Help us, O Lord, to know the things that are unseen and eternal, and to account them the abiding realities of life.

Give us, O Lord, a right judgement, that we may pursue true aims and serve great causes.

Grant us, O Lord, that with abiding power Thy law may be written in our hearts.

Grant, O Lord, that in the use of money and of time we may recognise our stewardship and our responsibility before Thee.

Hasten, if it may be, O Lord, Thy work of creation that man may be fashioned ever more and more into the likeness of Thy Son.

Teach us, O Lord, how to work with Thee in Thy great work of creation.

May Christ be for us the Lord of life, and in His Light may we seek the life that is life indeed.

May we come, O Lord, to know the Mind of Christ, and may His Spirit dwell in us.

Teach us, O Lord, so to witness to Christ by our lives that others may find in us a true witness to Thee.

The Grace was followed by silence, in which the congregation were asked to pray that the church in the diocese may become a fitter instrument of His purpose, and that we may be more truly of the Body of Christ.

Special intercessions for the work in hand followed later.

When the procession took place, and was carried through with perfect order, the church presented a remarkable and beautiful spectacle. The parish parties were led by their churchwardens carrying their staffs. Sidesmen carrying the gifts followed the parish banner. Scouts and Guides in uniform, G.F.S. representatives, in white dresses and blue veils, marched with their colour parties. Old age was represented by a party of women from Highbury Home, and early childhood by Infant and Sunday Schools. Mothers' Unions, Bible Classes and Catechisms all had their part. The processions began at the east end of the north and south aisles, converged under the tower, parties from each alternately passed up the centre of the church and, after presenting gifts, passed right and left to return to their places. The church was filled with three moving streams of colour. No one could miss the central purpose that the service was a service of offering. Our Bishop was there, of course, to receive the gifts and to preach the sermon. When we returned to the vestry he said, referring to the procession of offering, 'Well, if I were a schoolboy I should say "this has been a good show".'

Our first years at Moseley were busy but uneventful.

The parish was well organised, but we added one or two activities. My first curate had seen much service in France, Gallipoli, Egypt and Palestine, and had been twice mentioned in despatches. He brought with him a wife who was greatly liked. When he passed on to an Indian chaplaincy he left behind him two organisations which have been of great service: one was a promising troop of scouts, the other, which was not parochial, was Toc H. which has flourished greatly, and of which he was one of the founders.

Later the scouts were brought to a very high state of discipline and efficiency by a young schoolmaster, a Mr. Chedzoy, who came from Radstock to a mastership in a Council School on the borders of Moseley parish. His father had advised him to get in touch with me on his arrival in Birmingham. Unhappily, the war robbed us of his help all too soon.

During the war Convocation still met, and I attended almost all its sittings. I made one big effort myself to make the co-operation of the different bodies of Christians more real and effective. The Lower House of

Convocation debated at considerable length a resolution I moved, which was seconded by the Archdeacon of Loughborough, but it failed completely. Happily, our Archbishop William Temple in his own wise way, considerably increased the possible co-operation between the churches by uniting the small existing committees with increased powers, but I suppose that even now a large body of the clergy do nothing effective in trying to realise co-operation between the scattered fragments of Christianity in their own parishes. Even the menace of Russian communism does not seem to make them realise the dangers we are in 'by reason of our unhappy divisions.' My membership of Convocation from 1933 to 1943, when I resigned on leaving the diocese, as a byproduct, enabled me to increase greatly my knowledge of London. When the evenings were light, I used, as soon as the House rose, to go off exploring along the river. Sometimes I picked up an unexpected companion who asked if he might join me. One notable evening I saw a row boat coming in from the Pool of London. I called out to the waterman, 'Have you finished your job?' 'Yes,' he replied. 'What about taking me out?' 'Jump in,' he answered. We pushed out through a delightful flock of swans, the King's birds, and then through a flotilla of moored barges. I was for the first time afloat on the Pool of London in a row boat. For half an hour or more we rowed about at will between London Bridge and the Tower Bridge. Big shipping in the old days came no higher up the river than London Bridge. 'Below it a forest of masts covered the Pool of London, with which no scene in the world, save Amsterdam, could compare.' So said Trevelyan (English Social History. 336). William Dunbar burst into poetry in honour of the Thames: 'Above all rivers the river hath renown, Whose beryll streams, pleasant and preclair, Under the lusty walls runneth down;

Where many a swan doth swym with winges fair;

Where many a barge doth sail and row with care,

Where many a ship doth rest with top royal.

O town of towns! patron and not compare, London thou art the flour of cities all.'

On one delightful evening, I walked through that street of Rotherhithe which passes the parish church, and has short alleys every here and there running down to the river. On a piece of staging, near to an airhole of the tunnel under the Thames, a man with a wheelbarrow hard by had in his hand three or four lengths of that instrument which is used for clearing drains. I drew near and asked him what he was doing. 'I'm catching bits of wood,' he said. 'There's one coming,' and he pointed up the stream at one that, assisted by the tide which was running out swiftly, was rapidly approaching. As his quarry came within reach, he guided it with his drain cleaner so that it would pass under the staging just below his feet, and there he caught it. He held it up for a moment, just as a fisherman will hold up a big trout, and measured it with his eye, and then put it in the wheelbarrow. If the piece were too long for the wheelbarrow he would cut it with a saw which he had with him. A policeman, who was standing by the airshaft of the tunnel hard by, joined us. He was really a schoolmaster, in the police force for the war only, and a very intelligent and well-informed man. He pointed out many interesting things, and while we talked another police officer joined us, and invited us to walk his round with him. I gladly accepted and we sauntered around the poor burnt-out docks of Rotherhithe with their attractive names—Lavender Pond, Acorn Pond, Greenland Dock, Quebec Dock, Russia Dock, Lady Dock, and the like. But why 'Pond'? Does the name descend from the days when they were really ponds? But my guide had his eyes also on things beyond the reach of steam or sails. He was a churchwarden of Rotherhithe, and Rotherhithe church had a ghost. The ghost, he said, is that of an Indian Prince—(note: probably Prince Lee Boo of the Pelew Islands, d.1781)—who for some reason elected to live in Rotherhithe, and for some other reason, also unknown to me, died or was put to death in the vestry of Rotherhithe church. It all happened about 1800, and his ghost is said to walk. My companion and his other warden determined on the appropriate night to sit up in the vestry, and if possible meet this apparition. They sat up all night, but perhaps because one of the churchwardens was a policeman the ghost did not appear. Another night I walked from Stepney to St. Paul's and then on to my hotel in Bloomsbury. It was a weird walk. I hardly saw a soul the whole way, not even an Air-raid Warden, though no doubt plenty were at hand behind shuttered windows. I passed along the old Radcliffe Highway and never saw even a drunk. It recalled to mind a story told me by one of my former churchwardens. In early days he had served in the Merchant Service, and one early morning in Radcliffe Highway a man passed him, running for all he was worth to his ship, stark naked, except for a newspaper which he held in front of him.

No Germans came over that night. The approach to St. Paul's by a street I had never seen less than thronged was almost uncanny. I saw no living being, and not a light showed.

I reached my hotel in Bloomsbury about eleven o'clock, feeling as though I had passed a Dead Men's London.

What always impresses me was the friendliness of everybody in London. From Greenwich and the Isle of Dogs I now know something of it to Battersea Bridge. My rambles nearly always have a special feature. Today I went to the Isle of Dogs. We passed an ancient gateway. The conductor was disengaged so I asked him what the gate was. He shook his head. A negro on a seat in front on the other side turned his black and smiling face and said, 'That gate is St. John's Gate, a gate of the old City.' The conductor looked crestfallen and muttered explanations. In another bus I asked the sombre faced conductress if this bus would take me to the park in the Isle of Dogs, as I wanted to see the view of Greenwich College across the river. Her dark-complexioned face lit up with a cheery smile. It had never occurred to her that there was anything special to see from the gardens of the Isle of Dogs, but I had awakened her interest, and she stood by me and chatted whenever possible. I returned with the same conductress and she took care of me as if I were halt or blind, and when we said 'goodbye' she almost lifted me out of the bus, guided me to the pavement, and left me with many injunctions meant to safeguard my future safety. Though she was dark and sombre in expression, the change was wonderful when she began to smile.

CHAPTER SIXTEEN

SERMONS AND UNITY

One of the greatest hopes and prayers of my life has been for the reunion of Christendom, and especially for what must surely be a first step—the restoration of the unity of British Christianity, which is of far more practical moment to the cause of Christ than agreements with churches far from us, however desirable these rapprochements are. Britain could be, I believe, the strongest Christian centre in the world, if only reunion could be brought about with its repercussions in the Commonwealth, and the United States. That hope at the moment seems doomed to failure. Archbishop Temple, the great leader of the movement, is dead. The opponents of reunion have turned their thoughts to Rome, and while so many are now prepared to accept episcopacy as the only possible system of Church government for a reunited church, they are trying to tack on to it a doctrine of episcopacy which is very different from the acceptance of the fact—and it is never likely to receive general acceptance either within or without the church. That God is a Giver of Grace, and that those who seek it sincerely will find it, is common ground. That a great symbolic action at a most solemn moment of life can bring a new consciousness of the fellowship of the Holy Spirit and of the strength that flows from it, is a doctrine that few probably would dispute, but why drag the question further. Would that men could agree to accept great facts like Episcopacy or the Sacraments and, while free to hold theories they like of them, and to discuss as much as they choose, be content to refrain from trying to make their theories into religious tests. Theological colleges probably were a great gain when first founded. They seem now to lie at the root of many of our troubles. They are largely attached to church parties, which represent opinion narrower than the foundation of the Church of England. They are not normally and with exceptions the meeting ground as they should be of men of all kinds of views, where sympathies may be widened and understanding deepened, but where men are to be formed as in a seminary.

I have never been able to understand why men and women, who are undoubtedly followers of Christ, so easily find it impossible to work in harmony and comradeship with those who fight under the same flag, and who if persecution arose would certainly be likely to suffer together for Him with us. Bishops seem to me an excellent method of government, so long as their rule is constitutional, but I have never felt myself to be altogether an alien from my non-conformist neighbours. Let us go as far as we can together, and work together as far as possible. I have admitted to Communion members of the Free Churches and even Roman Catholics, some of whom have found themselves happier with us. I have in my life always held that reunion will be born of growing friendliness and co-operation, and not from theological discussion. It will, as in the parable, be by following Christ that men will find themselves one flock, and not by our trying to drive each other into our own fold. My greatest public effort on behalf of Reunion was a complete failure at that moment. On January 22nd 1942 I moved in the Lower House of Convocation the following Resolution—'That this House requests His Grace to appoint a commission to explore the possibility of creating a common Christian front of those bodies that acknowledge the kinship of Christ, by way of a union by which each body retains its full freedom of self government, by what may be likened to Dominio Status, while trying to promote common action through a Standing

Committee.' The resolution was seconded by the Archdeacon of Loughborough (then Ven. W. J. Lyon) but found no support. The opposition was led by Prebendary E. D. Merritt, who had great influence in Convocation. He proposed to substitute the following as an amendment, the omission of all words after House, and the substitution of the following 'desires to impress upon all Christian people the need for earnest and unceasing prayer for the reunion of Christendom.' This evidently met with widespread approval among a large section of the house who seem always ready for words but dread action. The Provost of Coventry was astonished that there had not yet been mentioned in the debate the existence of the Commission of the Churches for International Friendship and Social Responsibility. The Provost of Portsmouth was disappointed that no mention had been made of the World Council of Churches, and moved that the following words be added to the motion and the following resolution was then passed— 'That this House places on record its thankfulness for the co-operation, which has already been achieved and desires to impress upon all Christian people the need for earnest and unceasing prayer for the reunion of Christendom and it further commends the work of the Commission of the Churches for

International Friendship and Social Responsibility through which Christian bodies combine officially for common action.' The Prolocutor said he thought that members would agree that they had had a very interesting and important debate. That the House was interested is undoubtedly true, but how far it had any results is difficult to judge. It may well have contributed to the notable resolution in the Church Assembly of June 18th 1942, when the Bishop of Chichester moved and the Provost of Portsmouth seconded the following resolution 'That this Assembly approves the scheme for amalgamating the Council of Christian Faith and Common Life, the Commission of the Churches for International Friendship and Social Responsibility and the British Section of the World Conference of Faith and Order in a single body to be called the World Council of Churches.' The same kind of opposition began to manifest itself. Then the Archbishop of Canterbury asked the Bishop of London to take his place in the chair, and then gave emphatic support to the resolution. The house of Bishops and the house of Laity created a more favourable atmosphere for a forward move and the motion was put and carried. Its further history I do not know, but at any rate the course of unity and common action reaching out towards reunion has a definite organ, and that organ has a name which indicates its purpose, 'The British Council of Churches'. It is my conviction that while no reunion can be complete which does not include the Roman Catholic and the Orthodox Church and Lutherans, our first duty is to our own people. We must try to repair, so far as the breaches in our own body which have taken place since the Reformation. We shall then be in a much better position to move towards the next objective.